NCERT Workboook

Mathematics III

Collection of Worksheets and References for Students of Class III

Chandan Sukumar Sengupta

Creative Mathematics Series

NCERT Mathematics Workbook III

Collection of Worksheets and References for Students of Class III

ISBN: 9798413343494

Imprint: Independently published

This workbook is designed to equip students of class 3 of different curriculum framework for enabling them to acquire desired level of mathematical skills as pepr the standards prescribed for that particular level.

This workbook contains some activity sheets and reference worksheets suitable for the students of Grade 3. It is also suitable for aspirants preparing for Olympiads and other such enrichment activities.

Answer sheets with explanations are there in a separate sheet. It will enable parents and teachers for organizing the task in a better way. I am confident enough about the competence of fellow students having willingness to move up to the final stage of the Mathematics Enrichment Activities of various stages. There are different worksheets in accord to the time of studies that can be assigned to the fellow student. Answers are in a separate sheet paper that can be kept at different place. Parents and teachers use this book of activities to develop interest of students on mathematical as well as analytical skills.

For Students

We expect a kind of understanding from students of Grade 3 of the National Curriculum. The fellow student should understand the number system and related operations. There are some relationships exist in between number systems of various types. We often come across four different number system in computer Science. For the class works and mathematical operations of Grade 4 we restrict our discussion to decimal system only.

I hope the kind of effort and combination of problems might enhance the knowledge base of our fellow students.

For Parents

Questions are there without respective answers. It can be obtained from the source. There exists a plan of fulfilling dual purpose of the effort. These sets can be utilized to engage a student for working out the possible outputs without being inflicted primarily with answers.

If answers are provided alongside the questions then the material will fulfill half of the purpose. It cannot contingent for overcoming the problems and also cannot facilitate in skill enhancement efforts.

Set of questions can be used for the purpose of assessing skill acquisition process and also can be assigned to the ward by parents and guide.

Chandan Sukumar Sengupta

Author

.

This workbook is dedicated to the fellow students of class III.

Contents

Foreword

We expect a kind of understanding from students of Grade 3 of the National Curriculum. The fellow student should understand the number system and related operations. There are some relationships exist in between number systems of various types. We often come across four different types of number system in computer Science. For the class works and mathematical operations of Grade 3 we restrict our discussion to decimal system only. In actual format all numbers are decimal numbers as we express 3 as 3.0000 and ½ as 0.5. This mechanism should be dislayed roperly for enabling the fellow student to grasp through mathematical operations as per need.

I hope the kind of effort and combination of problems might enhance the knowledge base of our fellow students.

For Parents

Questions are there without respective answers. It can be obtained from the source. There exists a plan of fulfilling dual purpose of the effort. These sets can be utilized to engage a student for working out the possible outputs without being inflicted primarily with answers.

If answers are provided alongside the questions then the material will fulfill half of the purpose. It cannot contingent for overcoming the problems and also cannot facilitate in skill enhancement efforts.

Set of questions can be used for the purpose of assessing skill acquisition process and also can be assigned to the ward by parents and guides.

It is not mandatory to go through all sets of problems, but not to skip any of the problems is recommended for assuring the perfect skill acquisition.

Author
February 2022

Basic Concepts

1. The number system which deals with 10 different digits is called decimal system.

   324,432,232 is the number represented by using digits from the collection of 10 different digits, such as 0,1,2,3,4,5,6,7,8 and 9.

2. Expanded form of 213,324,543 can be expressed as follows:

213,324,543	=	___X 1,00,000,000
	+	1 X 10,000,000
	+	3 X 1,000,000
	+	___X 100,000
	+	___X 10,000
	+	___X 1,000
	+	___X 100
	+	___X 10
	+	___X 1

3. We can construct 6 different three digit numbers by using digits 2, 4 and 8 only once.

   Six such numbers constructed by using digits 3, 6 and 9 are:

   369, 396, 639, 693, 963 and 936

4. There are two different types of numeration, one is Indo-Arabic system of numeration and the another one is International system of numeration. All numbers can be expressed in any of the given system of numeration.

   The given number   : 125894534

   Indo- Arabic Numeration   : 12,58,94,534

   Twelve crore, fity-eight lakh ninety four thousand five hundred and thirty four

   The given number   : 125,894,534

   One hundred twenty five million, eight hundred ninety –four thousand five hundred and thirty four.

5. Sum total of all the interior angles of a triangle is 180^0 .

6. Hour hand, minute hand and second hand of a clock completes one rotation by forming a complete angle at the center (360^0).

7. The greatest five digit number without repeating any digit twice is 98,765.

8. The smallest five digit number without repeating any digit twice is 10,234.

9. 3 must be subtracted from the greatest five digit number to make the value divisible by 4.

$$[\ 99,999 - 3 = 99,996 ; \quad \frac{99,996}{4} = 24,999 \quad ;]$$

10. Numbers having only 2 factors, 1 and the number itself, are called prime numbers. 1 is not a prime number. 2 is the smallest and only even prime number.

11. Any natural number and whole number can be represented in a number line.

12. All basic shapes having length and breadth are called 2 dimensional shapes.

13. All basic shapes having length breadth and height are called 3 dimensional shapes.

14. All basic shapes occuly a definite space.

15. All 2 dimensional shapes lie on a definite plane.

16. Two planes meet through a straight line.

17. All polygons have a definite numbers of sides that encloses a definite area of a plane. Triangle is the smallest polygon having three sides, three vertices and three angles. Sum total of all the interior angles of a triangle is 180^0. Some total of all the interior angles of othe polygon are calculated on the basis of non-overlaing triangles that can be accommodated inside the polygon. A rectangle, for an example, can accommodate two non-overlappping triangles. That is why sum-total of interior angles of a rectangle is 180^0 X 2 = 360^0 .

Content Areas

1. Basic operations of Natural numbers up to seven digits.

2. Standard forms and expanded forms (Indian and International System).

3. Basic operations related to fraction, decimal and percentage.

4. Shapes and their properties: Triangles, squares, rectangle, parallelogram, trapezium,

5. Lines and angles.

6. Measurements of Linght, mass, time, weight, temperature etc.

7. Factors, Multiples and Prime Factorisations.

8. HCF and LCM

9. Area and Perimeter (Triangles, Quadrilatrals and Circles)

10. Volume and Surface areas (Cube, Cuboids, Spheres Cones)

11. Basic operations related to fractions and decimals.

12. Bar Graphs, Pie Charts and Average.

13. Rays, Lines and Line Segments.

14. Intersecting and parallel lines.

15. Combined operations and unitary methods.

16. Basic ideas of polygons and some important properties of it.

Notes and References

Some of the note and References regarding core of the mathematical

1. Numbers having only two factors, such as and the nuber itself, is called a prime number.

2. Numbers having more than two factors are called composite numbers.

3. All the even numbers are multiples of 2.

4. All odd numbers are not necessarily multiples of 3. Only numbers in which sum total of digits is a multiple of three is divisible by 3.

5. Prime numbers between 1 and 100 are : 2, 3, 5, 7, 11, 13, 17, 19, 23, 29, 31, 37, 41, 43, 47, 53, 59, 61, 67, 71, 73, 79, 83, 89 and 97.

6. Sum total of all the interior angles of a triangle is 180^0.

7. Sum total of all the exterior angles of any polygon is always 360^0 .

8. Any natural number and whole number can be represented on a number line.

9. There are principally two types of decimals: terminating and nonterminating types. Non-terminating types are further two types: Repeating and nonrepeating types.

10. Counting numbers along with zero are called whole numbers.

11. All the whole numbers along with negative numbers are called integers. (Example: -3, -2, -1, 0, 1, 2 etc.)

12. A number representing part of a whole is called a fraction.

13. $\frac{1}{2}, \frac{1}{3}, \frac{1}{4}$ *etc are called unit fractions.*

14. $\frac{11}{12}, \frac{21}{33}, \frac{12}{14}$ *etc are called proper fractions.*

These types of fractions have numerators less than denominators.

15. $\frac{19}{12}, \frac{31}{23}, \frac{41}{24}$ *etc are called improper fractions. These types of fractions have numerators*

greater than denominators.

16. $3\frac{1}{2}$, $21\frac{1}{3}$, $4\frac{1}{4}$ *etc are called mixed fractions.*

17. A cuboid has six faces , 12 edges and 8 corners. Edges of opposite faces are parallel to each other.

18. All the faces of a cube represent congruent squares having area of equal magnitude.

19. Percentage is a special type of fraction and also is a special type of decimal.

    For example: 25% = $\frac{25}{100} = 0.25$;

20. There are different types of Prism. Names of prisms are coined on the basis of the nature of bases.

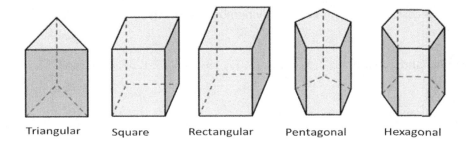

| Triangular | Square | Rectangular | Pentagonal | Hexagonal |

21. A Net for rectangular, square prism and octahedron :

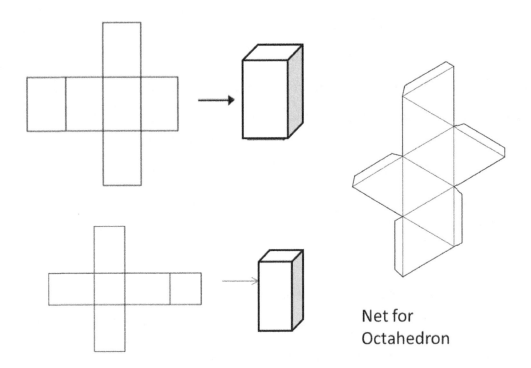

Net for
Octahedron

1. Selected Worksheets

You can start typing out or copy-pasting the first chapter of your book here.

Worksheet 1

1. A teacher purchased three types of pens.

   6 boxes of red pens with 40 pens in each box

   5 boxes of blue pens with 20 pens in each box

   Which number is closest to the total pens?

   A: 250   B: 350C: 400D: 450

2. All the three digit numbers formed by using digits 4, 3 and 0. If you arrange these numbers in ascending orders then _____a_____ comes in the second position and ___b___ comes at last.

   A: a =304 b = 430, B: a= 340, b= 403

   C: a =340 b = 430, D: a = 304 b = 430

3. Mr Jordon prepares to put fencing around his rectangular kitchen garden of width 95 m and the length 105 m. How long fencing wires does he need?

   A: 190 m   B: 200 m

   C: 210 m   D: 400 m

4. There are ____ diagonals in a Pentagon.

5. Find the digit present in the thousands place in the product

   $(11011 \div 11) \times 7000 =$ _____

   A: 1   B: 11   C: 121   D: 111

6. There are total _____ lines of symmetry in a regular hexagon.

   A: 18 B: 9   C: 12 D: 6

7. Sum total of the smallest and the greatest four digit numbers formed by without repeating any digits twice is _____ more than the smallest five digit number.

   9,876 + 1,023 = _____.

   A: 763   B: 899C: 989D: 1209

8. A teacher purchased three types of pens.

   6 boxes of red pens with 40 pens in each box

   5 boxes of blue pens with 20 pens in each box

   Which number is closest to the total pens?

   A: 250   B: 350C: 400D: 450

9. All the three digit numbers formed by using digits 4, 3 and 0. If you arrange these numbers in ascending orders then _____a_____ comes in the second position and ___b___ comes at last.

10. Mr Jordon prepares to put fencing around his rectangular kitchen garden of width 95 m and the length 105 m. How long fencing wires does he need?
    A: 190 m   B: 200 m   C: 210 m   D: 400 m

11. Half of the half of 98 = _____ of 196.

12. Sum total of all the numbers formed by using digits 1,3 and 0 only once is _____.

13. _____ is the only number which is a factor of all the numbers.

14._____ is the predecessor of smallest six digit odd number.

15. Mandela wanted to add three digit greatest number to another number to obtain a five digit smallest number. He has added _____ to the third multiple of 333.

16._____ is the predecessor of 4 digit greatest even number.

17. At 1 O Clock and 11 O Click both hour hand and minute hand of a clock makes an angle of ___a_____ which is __b__ of a complete angle.

      A: a= 90^0 b = $1/4^{th}$ B: a= 180^0 b = $1/2^{nd}$

      C: a= 270^0 b = $1/3^{rd}$ D: a= 30^0 b = $1/12^{th}$

18. One fourth of a scale is equal to one tenth of another scale. For measuring a ribbon of 8m the longer scale is used ten times. Find the length of the shorter scale.

    A: 1 m   B: 2 mC: 3 m   D: 4 m

19. Compare the place value of 3 in 2,309 and 3,283. Find the difference of both the place values of 3. The difference is the _(____) th multiple of 100.

    A: 27   B: 30   C: 28   D: 35

20.. _____ is the difference between 4th multiple of 9 and 6th multiple of 100.

    A: 636   B: 536   C: 564   D: 546

21._____ is the only even prime number.

22. 2, 3, _____ and _____ are first four prime numbers.

23. Add: 100 + 3 tens + 32 hundreds + 12 ones = __.

24. A _____ has one endpoint and it can be extended endlessly in one direction.

Worksheet 2

1. The floor of a room a hotel is 12 m long and 10 m wide. 45 tiles of 1 m square was in stock. Tiles come in market in pack of ten tiles. How many more 1m square tiles does the manager need to completely cover the floors of three such rooms?

    I: 15 tiles more than 30 full pack

    II: 5 tiles more than 31 full pack

    III: 25 tiles more than 29 full pack

    IV: 50 tiles more than 25 full pack

    Select your answers

    A: Only I   B: Only II   C: I, II and III D: Only IV

2. Multiples of 16 are also multiples of 4 and 8, but all multiples of _____ and _____ are not multiples of 16.

3. A football is 27 times heavier than a tennis ball. A tennis ball is 9 times lighter than a rubber ball. _____ rubber balls will be equal of three footballs.

4. A regular pentagon has __a___ lines of symmetry less than a hexagon. It has _____b _____ lines of symmetry more than an equilateral triangle. Both square and equilateral triangle has __ c__ lines of symmetry in all.

	a	b	c
A:	1	2	7
B:	2	4	8
C:	1	2	3
D:	2	4	6

5. Other two angles of a triangle are 2/3rd and 1/3rd of a right angle respectively. Find the measure of all the interior angles of a triangle.

6. Ravi is 3 years older than Mallika but 2 years younger than Kamal. Who is youngest among them? Arrange their names in ascending order of their age.

7. Total cost of 5 pens and 3 pencils is Rs. 85. Find the total cost of 1 pen and 1 pencil if total cost of 3 pens and 2 pencils is Rs. 61.

8. What must be added to make 10,982 divisible by 11?

9. Find a factor of 121 which is also a factor of 2020.

10. Difference of digits of a two digit number is 7. if digits are reversed then sum total of both the number becomes the predecessor of the three digit smallest number. Find the second multiple of this number.
   A: 45 B: 18 C: 36 D: 81

11. On Monday, Meena wanted to meet a reporter at 11.30 am sharp. Due to traffic problems she was 25 min late. Mohini left 15 min after Meena. Rebeka reported her arrival time 55 min more than that of Mohini. At what time did Rebeka reach?
   A: 1:30 pm   B: 1:40 pm

   C: 11:55 am   D: 12:40 pm

12. Observe the following statements. It describes the population of cats, dogs and rabbits in a city duly recorded last year.
   Number of Cats < Number of Dogs

   Number of Dogs > Number of Rabbits

   Which could be the number of cats and dogs?

	Cats	Dogs	Rabbits
A	192	232	176
B	306	127	176
C	432	542	675
D	541	329	767

13.. A wall mount clock takes 2 seconds to ring two bells at 2 O Clock. Calculate the time taken by the same clock to ring seven bells at 7 O Clock.

A: 14 seconds   B: 7 seconds C: 12 seconds   D: 10 seconds

14. Complete the following:

1, 4, 9, __a___, __b___, ___c___;

Options	a	b	c
A:	16	25	36
B:	21	27	29
C:	12	15	19

15. The digit at one's place of a number which is 3 less than the third multiple of 1427.

A: 6   B:7   C: 8   D: 9

16. There are two combinations of packs containing pens and pencils. Packet one containing 6 pens and 5 pencils costs Rs 128. Packet B containing 5 pens and 6 pencils costs Rs 103. Calculate the cost of a new pack containing 10 pens and 10 pencils of such type?

A: Rs. 250   B: Rs. 120   C: Rs. 135   D: Rs. 210

17. Last Thursday in the calendar it was 27th February 2020. The forthcoming Thursday will be _____March 2020.

A: 4   B: 5   C: 6   D: 7

18. The product of 10th multiple of 11 and the 7th multiple of 109 has _____ at its one's place.

A: 0   B: 1   C: 2   D: 3

19. 121, 169 and 219 have following things in common:

I. All these numbers are square numbers.

II. These are square numbers of odd primes.

III. These numbers have equal numbers of prime factors.

Select which of the statements mentioned above are true.

A: Only I   B: Only II

C: Both I and III   D: All I, II and III

20. _____ is the sixth multiple of only even prime number.

21. 36 has _____ factors in all:

Statement : 36 is a composite numbers.

Reason   : 36 has more than two factors.

A: The given reason is appropriate.

21

B: The given reason is not correct.

C: The given reason requires more explanation.

D: Both the statement and reason are wrong.

22. Observe following statements:

I: 2 is an even prime number.

II: 2 has no factors other than 1 and the number itself.

III: 2 has another factor which is also a factor of all the other natural numbers.

IV: All the other even numbers are multiples of 2.

Select which of the statements mentioned above are true.

A: Only I   B: Only II

C: Only I and III   D: All

23. Rijuana dirves 185 miles , 439 miles and 219 miles respectively during three consecutive days of a trip. The best estimation of the total distance covered by Rijuana will be:

    a. 150 + 400 + 200   miles

    b. 200 + 400 + 200   miles

    c. 200 + 450 + 200   miles

    d. 200 + 450 + 250   miles

24. A regular pentagon can have _____ lines of symmetry which is _____ more than the lines of symmetry present in a regular quadrilateral.

25. ___ , _____ and _____ are three prime numbers located in between 1 and 6.

26. The smallest 4 digit number divisible exactly by 9 = _____.

Worksheet 3

1. One sixth of sixty million is equal to _____ ten thousand.

2. Ravi compared the place value of 5 and 8 in the following number and found that the product of both the place value is _____.

   456.3087

3. Observe the number pattern and complete the same:

   1 X 1   = 1

   11X 11   = 121

   ___ X ___   = 12321;

   1111 X _____   = _____;

4. Simplify the following:

   a. 10001 X 9999 = _____;

   b. 15 hundreds + 15 tens + 15 ones + 15 tenths = _____.

5. Complete the statement:

   a. Digit 7 comes for _____ times while writing all the numbers from 1 to 100.

   b. The smallest possible six digit number divisible exactly by 9 is _____.

   c. Rishabh can collect three fruits in a scond. He can collect _____ fruits from the garden in 2 hours.

6. Hiralaal drives a car up to 120 miles by consuming 10 litres of fuel. He can drive _____ miles by consuming 23 litres of fuel.

7. Observe the pattern and complete the given statements.

   a) $(1 + 2 + 3 + \ldots + 100) = (100 + 1) \times (100/2) =$ _____.

   b) $(1 + 2 + 3 + \ldots + 1000) =$ _____ X _____ = _____.

   c) $(1 + 2 + 3 + \ldots + 10000) =$ _____ X _____ = _____.

d) $(1 + 2 + 3 + ... + 600) =$ _____ X _____ = _____.

8. The number given below is a multiple of 8. Provide the missing digit of tens place to make the statement true.

Ten Thousands
Thousands
Hundreds
Tens
Ones

3   6   8   —   2

9. Write the following number in standard form and also check its divisibility by 11. If it is not divisible by 11 then what least number must be added to it or subtracted from it to make it divisible by 11?

11 thousands + 11 hundreds + 11 tens + 110 ones + 11 ten thousands

10. Consider the following information.

A number is divisible by 4 if number formed by the combination of digits present at tens place and ones place become divisible by 4. For example , **124**; 1,243,543,2**16** and other such numbers are multiples of 4.

Now solve the following:

What least number can be subtracted from the greastest even number of six digits to make the value a multiple of 4?

11. Ruchira observed that just after adding a thousand to a five digit greatest possible number it becomes a multiple of 8 Find the number.

[Solution: 99,902]

12. What least number must be added to a greatest five digit multiple of 8 to make it a multiple of 11?

13. In a special way we can find the product of following numbers by rearranging them and after that by applying identities.

$101 \times 99 = (100 + 1)(100-1) = 100^2 - 1^2 = 10,000 -1 = 9,999$

Similarly find the product of following numbers:

    a. 10001×9999 b. $8,004 \times 7,996$

    c: $10,003 \times 9,997 - 1003 \times 997$

    d: $[51 \times 49 - 102 \times 98][105 \times 95 - 106 \times 94]$

14. Is there any pair of number having LCM 1331 and HCF 333?

15. A four digit multiple of 3 is such that after reversing all digits the difference of a thousand is obtained. Find all such combination of digits. Also count the number of such options which is possible.

[one such option is 2,001 and 1,002]

16. Observe the number pattern ...

    1, 1, 2, 3, 5, _____, 13, 21, _____, _____

    a. Provide missing numbers.

    b. Provide seventh number of the series.

    c. Sum total of fourth and sixth value = _____

17. What least number must be added to a seven digit smallest number to make it divisible by 11?

18. Form the greatest and smallest possible five digit numbers without repeating any of the digits twice. Also find their sum total.

19. A number becomes less than a hundred after adding 204 to it. Find the number.

20. Find the value: $\left(1 + \dfrac{1}{2}\right)\left(1 + \dfrac{1}{3}\right) \ldots\ldots \left(1 + \dfrac{1}{1560}\right)$

[Solution : 8]

Worksheet 4

1. Rani is buying light bulbs for her Christmas decorations. She buys 1020 but when she gets to the cash, she has to put back 3 hundred 13 because they are broken. How many light bulbs does Marie buy?

2. There are two combinations of packs containing Cakes and Biscuits. Packet one containing 6 cakes and 5 biscuitsls costs Rs 128. Packet B containing 5 cakes and 6 biscuits costs Rs 103. Calculate the cost of a new pack containing 10 cakes and 10 biscuits of such type?

   A: Rs. 250   B: Rs. 120   C: Rs. 135   D: Rs. 210

3. Last Thursday in the calendar it was 27th February 2020. The forthcoming Thursday will be _____ March 2020.

   A: 4   B: 5   C: 6   D: 7

4. The product of 10th multiple of 11 and the 7th multiple of 109 has _____ at its one's place.
   A: 0   B: 1   C: 2   D: 3

5. If 36 X 121 = 4,356 , then :
   a) 36X10 X 100 =
   b) 36X 400 =
   c) 36 X 200 =
   d) 36 X 1,000 =

6. 121,121 ÷ 121 =

   A: 11   B: 101   C: 110D:1001

7. Product of all the factors of 6 = _____
   A: 36   B: 12   C: 18   D: 24

8. Some of the statements regarding prime and composite numbers are given below.

   I : 1 is not a prime *or* composite number.

   II : Two is the only even prime number.

   III: All odd numbers are not prime.

   IV: All composite numbers can be written as product of prime numbers.

   V: 101 has only two factors 1 and the number itself. That is why it is a prime number

   Which of the above statements are true?

   A: Only I   B: All   C: I, II and III D: Only II, III and IV

9. 121, 165 and 594 have following things in common:
   I. All these numbers are multiples of 11.

   II. These are square numbers and also are in a   pattern of incremental type. .

   III. Prime factors of these numbers are different.

   Select which of the statements mentioned above are true.

   A: Only I   B: Only II   C: Both I and III   D: All I, II and III

10. If we continue the following pattern:

    2,000 1,750 1,500 1,250 , a , b , c

    and a X b X c = d; then the digits at ones, tens and hundreds place of d respectively are

    A: 1,2,3   B: 2,1,3   C: 0, 0,0   D: 1, 1, 1

11. Observe the following numbers represented in expanded form.

    30,550   = 50 + a + 500

    809,100 = 800,000 + 100 + _b

    725,608 = 20,000 + 700,000 + 8 + c + 5,000

    I.   Numbers are represented in the International System.
    II.   All a, b and c are in thousands.
    III. Sum total of a, b and c exceeds 60,000.
    IV.   In ascending order c > b > a.
    V.   Which of the statements are true?

    A: I, II and IV   B: Only IV   C: None

12. Half a dozen banana is ___a ___ less than a score of it. Here a = _____
    A: 20   B: 14   C: 16   D: 20

13.. Observe factors of 12 and 36 ….

    Factors of 36 are   1,36,2,18,3,**12,6**,9,4

    Factors of   12 are 1,**12**, 2, **6** , 3, **4**,

    If common factors of 12 and 36 arranged from least to greatest are   a, b, c, and if a x b + c = d, then d = ____

    A: 24   B: 36   C: 72   D: 48

14.13. Height of a tree is 2 m more than a building but 3 m less than a telephone tower. If telephone tower is 50 m tall, then find the sum total of heights of all the three objects.

A: 212 m   B: 125 m

C: 142 m   D: 165 m

15. There are _____ diagonals in a rhombus.

16. Observe the following:

12,345 = P + 2,000 + 300 + 40 + 5;

29,658 = 20,000 + Q + R + 50 + 8;

P is _____ more than Q + R;

A: 4   B: 40   C: 400D: 4000

17. 3 less than 6,000 is added to a five digit greatest number. The sum total is then rounded up to nearest thousands. Find the value.

A: 16,000B: 60,000   C: 10,600   D: 16,200

18. 5th multiple of 600 and 6th multiple of 500 multiplied to obtain a value which is _____ less than the smallest 6 digit number.

A: 30,000B: 50,000   C: 40,000   D: 66,000

19.5. 100th multiple of the product of all the factors of 8 is _____ more than the 6th multiple of 1,000.

A: 200   B: 400 C: 500   D: 600

20. There are ___ faces , ____ edges and ____ vertices in a hexagonal Prism.

21. Temperature of a city increased by 5 ^{0} C last week. If a corresponding increase of temperature in ^{0} F is 1.8 times more than that of the value in ^{0} C , then find the value of such increase of temperature in ^{0} F

22. A: 18^0 F   B: 9^0 F C: 8.9^0 F   D: 6 ^{0} F

23. Half of a quarter of four digit smallest number exceeds the greatest two digit number by P. If we multiply P by half of it then the value represents a ____ multiple of 13.

A: 24   B: 25

C: 26   D: 27

24. Three consecutive multiples of 25 located in between 100 and 200 are _____, _____ and _____.

25. Sum total of half of a number and quarter of number is equal to 16 less than a hundred. Find the number.

26. 16 tenths + 21 hundredths + 101 thousandths = _____.

27. The smallest five digit multiple of 6 is _____ more than the smallest five digit number.

Worksheet 5

1. Write a number greater than 1, 50,000 by using digits 5, 4 and 2.

2. 324 thousands = _____ tens.

3. 32 crore = _____ thousands.

4. _____ crore is 400 greater than 99,99,600.

5. Write a number smaller than 39 lakhs by using digits 4, 3 and 8. Digits can be repeated.

6. Write the predecessor of 7 digit greatest number.

7. Calculate the sum total of place values of 3 in the following numbers

8. 34,55,67,505,   30,56,05,506 and 35,05,04,050

9. Difference of the place value and face value of 8 in 65,76,80,653, 78,806 and 48,65,678 = _____.

10. ____,00,00,000 = 18 crore.

11. Numbers divisible by 2 are also called _____ numbers.

12. ____ is the only even prime number.

13. All prime numbers have only _____ factors. ____ and the number itself.

14. Sum total of 2 eve numbers is always an _____ number.

15. Sum total of an even number and an odd number is always an _____ number.

16. A prime number between 95 and 100 = _____.

17. All the multiples of 8 are also multiples of 2 and _____.

18. All the multiples of ____ and 4 may or may not be a multiple of 8.

19. All the multiples of ___ and ____ are not necessarily multiples of 10.

20. All multiples of 10 are also multiples of _____ and _____.

Worksheet 6

1. What least number must be added to 109 to make it a multiple of 3?

2. Identify 4 pairs of twin prime numbers.

3. Find a pair of twin prime number whose sum total is 300.

4. Find the smallest possible sum total of a twin prime numbers which is also a multiple of 4.

5. How many twin primes are there in between 1 and 20?

6. Which prime numbers are predecessor and successor of 100?

7. Consecutive primes located before 15 are _____ and _____.

8. Add the following:

a) 123,433,540 + 32,435+ 324,435

b) 101,101 + 320,239 + 101,909 + 202,208

c) 3 million + 324 thousand + 324 hundred

d) 21 million + 213 thousand + 213

e) 21X 10,000 + 21 X 20,000 + 11X 10,000

f) 21X 10,000 + 21X 1,--- + 21X 100

g) 32 lakhs + 324 thousands + 21 hundreds + 21 tens

9. You are selling drinks at the school dance. You have a cooler, which holds 35 cups. The canteen gets busy and you lose track of how many cups you sold. You check and see that there are 17 cups left in the cooler. How many drinks must you have sold?

10. Rani is buying light bulbs for her Christmas decorations. She buys 1020 but when she gets to the cash, she has to put back 3 hundred 13 because they are broken. How many light bulbs does Marie buy?

11. There are two combinations of packs containing pens and pencils. Packet one containing 6 pens and 5 pencils costs Rs 128. Packet B containing 5 pens and 6 pencils costs Rs 103. Calculate the cost of a new pack containing 10 pens and 10 pencils of such type?

   A: Rs. 250   B: Rs. 120   C: Rs. 135   D: Rs. 210

12. Last Thursday in the calendar it was 27th February 2020. The forthcoming Thursday will be _____March 2020.

   A: 4   B: 5   C: 6   D: 7

13. The product of 10th multiple of 11 and the 7th multiple of 109 has _____ at its one's place.

   A: 0   B: 1   C: 2   D: 3

14. If 36 X 121 = 4,356 , then :

e) 36X10 X 100 =

f) 36X 400 =

g) 36 X 200 =

h) 36 X 1,000 =

i) 4,356 ÷ 121 =

j) 4,356 ÷ 36 =

k) 4,356 ÷ 18 =

15. Check the divisibility of 32,43,434 by 4, 8 and 11

16. Find a greatest 7 digit number which is divisible by both 4 and 8.

17. What must be added to 6 digit greatest number to make it divisible by 6?

18. All numbers are divisible by _____.

19. We cannot divide any number by _____.

Worksheet 7

1. Complete the following number pattern:

a) 88,_____, _____, _____, 33, _____. _____.

b) 121, _____, _____, _____, _____, 55, ____, _____, 22, 11

c) 12, ___, _____, 12,345, _____.

d) 10204, _____, _____, _____, _____ , 12,204, 12,404.

e) 144, _____, _____, _____, 96, 84 , _____, _____.

2. Add : MMDCXX + MCDXCLVI

3. Subtract: MMMCLX – MCMLXXXV

4. Arrange the following in ascending and descending order:

a) MDC, MCMLXV, MCDXCLV, MDLXVIII

b) XXII, XXXVIII, XCLXXVI, XVI

c) MMMCMXCIX, MMMXII, MMMCMXXII,

5. Compare:

a) MMMCMXCIX _____ MMMDCXCIX;

b) CMCCX _____ MCCX

c) XXIV _____XXXIII

6. Complete the following:

   36,653   = _____   + ___ + _____ +___ + _____.

7. 2,892   =   X 1000 + …. X 100   + …. X 10   + …….X 1

8. Complete the following:

a) _____ are what we can multiply to get numbers.

b) _____ are what we get after multiplying the number by any other number.

c) _____ is a factor of all the numbers.

d) All the numbers are one of the multiple of _____.

e) All _____ numbers have only two factors, 1 and the number itself.

f) 36 has _____ factors in all.

g) 36 has _____ prime factors in all.

h) All the factors of 18 are also _____ of 36, but all the _____ of 36 are not the factors of 18.

i) _____ are always greater than or equal to the number.

9. Multiples of 4 are also multiples of 2, but all multiples of 2 are not necessarily multiples of _____.

10. _____ is the smallest three digit number divisible by 8.

11. Find outer boundary of the given figure.

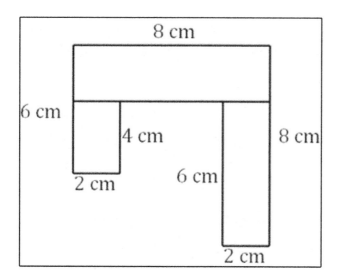

12. Rijuana observed that if she rides 12 miles more then she cross the destiny by 3 miles and if she rides 8 miles more then she will remain a mile away from the destiny. What is the exact distance she has to cover for reaching her destiny?

13. The sum total of the greatest even number of fur digits and a smallest odd number of five digits = _____.

Worksheet 8

1. Find the digit present in the thousands place in the product

2. $(11011 \div 11) \times 7{,}000 = $ _____

3. $(121 \div 11) \times 8{,}000 = $ _____

4. $(12310 \div 11) \times 9{,}000 = $ _____

5. $(12221 \div 121) \times 6{,}000 = $ _____

6. 2. Sum total of the smallest and the greatest four digit numbers formed by without repeating any digits twice is _____ more than the smallest five digit number.

7. 432 hundreds + 232 tens + 32 ones = _____ .

8. $9{,}876 + 1{,}023 = $ _____ .

9. Difference of digits of a two digit number is 7. if digits are reversed then sum total of both the number becomes the predecessor of the three digit smallest number. Find the second multiple of this number.

10. Compare the place value of 3 in 2,309 and 3,283. Find the difference of both the place values of 3. The difference is the _(____) th multiple of 100.

11. 121, 169 and 219 have following things in common:

    I. All these numbers are square numbers.

    II. These are square numbers of odd primes.

    III. These numbers have equal numbers of prime factors.

    Select which of the statements mentioned above are true.

    A: Only I   B: Only II   C: Both I and III   D: All I, II and III

12. Complete the Prime factorisation:

    a) 141   = _____   X___;

    b) 84 = _____;

    c) 363 = _____ X _____ ;

    d) $3{,}000 = 2 \times 2 \times 2 \times$ _____

    e) $729 = $ __ X __X___ X ___X___;

f) _____ = 89 X 11

13. In the calculation table depicted below numbers are related to each other. Find their inter relations and also identify missing numbers.

14. 32 X 10,000 = _____ X 16 = _____ X 8.

15. 8th multiple of of 16 is _____ multiple of 32.

16. 9th multiple of 11 is _____ multiple of 9.

17. After subtracting _____ we can obtain 3rd multiple of 13 from the 4th multiple of 10.

18. Complete the following:

a) 1, 4, 9, __i___, __ii___, ___iii___;

b) i X ii + iii = _____

c) 1, 8, 27, _____, _____ , _____ .

d) 121, _____, _____ , _____ 161.

e) 64, _____, _____ , _____ , 16, 9.

19. Product of all the factors of 6 = _____

A: 36   B: 12

C: 18   D: 24

20. Some of the statements regarding prime and composite numbers are given below.

  I :   1 is not a prime **or** composite number.

  II :   Two is the only even prime number.

  III: All odd numbers are not prime.

  IV: All composite numbers can be written as

  product of prime numbers.

  V: 101 has only two factors 1 and the number itself. That is why it is a prime number

  Which of the above statements are true?

  A: Only I   B: All   C: I, II and III   D: Only II, III and IV

Worksheet 9

1. Temperature of a city increased by 5 ^{0} C last week. If a corresponding increase of temperature in ^{0} F is 1.8 times more than that of the value in ^{0} C , then find the value of such increase of temperature in ^{0} F

    A: 18^0 F   B: 9^0 FC: 8.9^0 F   D: 6 ^{0} F

2. A racing car covers 100 km in 2 hours and another 400 km 4 hours. The speed of the car during second time is _____ times more than that of the first time.

    A: 1   B: 2   C: 3   D: 4

3. The product of the place values of 5 in the following number is _____

    32,435

    A: 9,000   B: 90,000

    C: 9,00,000   D: 900

4. What must be added to 10932 to make it exactly divisible by 9?

5. $\dfrac{3}{6}, \dfrac{7}{6}, \dfrac{1}{6}, \dfrac{5}{6}, \dfrac{11}{6}$

    If we arrange these fractions in ascending order, then denominator of the product of 2nd and 3rd fraction in simplest form will be _____

    A: 12 B: 24 C: 36 D: 48

6. Half of one sixth of 72 is the _____ multiple of three.

7. A wire of a square sized shape of side 32 cm is reshaped to form a circle. Find the circumference of that circle. [Circumference of a circle is the outer boundary of a circle].

8. A solid cylinder has _____ flat faces and _____ curved faces.

9. The product of all the factors of 121 is _____ less than its greatest factor.

    A: 1   B: 11 C: 1,452   D: 1331

10. Two bells toll at an interval of 6 seconds and 8 seconds respectively. They toll together at 11:55 a.m. When do they toll together again for the second time?

A: 12:19 pm   B: 12:19 am C: 12: 24 pm

11. Ruchika observed that a 300 m long goods train is taking 45 seconds to cross a light-post. Find the average speed of that train. Also find the time taken by that train to cross a 1500 m long railway platform.

12. Compare the place value of 5 in 235,934 and 54,435. Find difference of both the place values.

13. A milk-dairy produces 25,545 liters of milk every day. It supplies 15,625 liters of milk to a milk-depot and the rest to the market. How much milk is supplied to the market?

14. The sum of two numbers is 94506. One of the numbers is 49605. Find the other number.

15. The sum of two numbers is 45650. One of the numbers is 22587. Find the other number. Which part of the sum is the given number?

16. There are 35,278 students in Class III, 32,184 students in Class IV and 25,375 students in Class V in the schools of a city. Find the total number of students reading in Classes III, IV and V. Among these students 60,324 are girls. Find the number of students who are boys.

17. A person had $ 197,865. He gave $ 50,753 to his wife and $ 75,928 to his son. The rest of the money he gave to his daughter. How much did the daughter get?

18. 14. What should be added to the sum of 3,46,068 and 3,24,263 to get the sum of 8,05,400?

19. There are 4021 students in a school. Each section can accommodate a maximum number of 25 students. There are equal number of students in each section, find their number in each section. Is there any section having less than 25 students? How many such sections are there?

20. Write in standard form:

32 tens + 54 hundreds + 121 ones = _____ .

Worksheet 10

1. Twice of one third of 39 = _____.

2. Which fraction of figure is shaded?

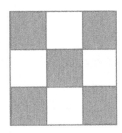   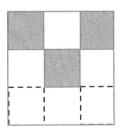

   I   II

3. _____ is the greatest two digit prime number.

4. _____ is the greatest possible even number of 5 digits which is also a common multiple of 2 and 4.

5. In her social studies report, Suzanne included a bar graph that showed the populations of different Native American nations in 1800. The interval she used was 2,000 people. If one nation had a population represented by 2.5 intervals, how many members of this nation existed in 1800?

6. Anthony emptied his coin bank and made a bar graph of the numbers of each type of coin. The interval he chose was 5 coins. If the graph showed 5 intervals of quarters, 2 intervals of dimes, 3 intervals of nickels, and 10 intervals of pennies, what was the total amount of money in his bank?

7. 54 tens + 32 hundreds + 43 = _____.

8. 24 tens + 121 tenths + 208 thusandths = _____.

9. Half of a quarter of 144 reduced to its tenth part = _____.

10. Quarter of a one sixth of 240,240 = _____.

Worksheet 11

1. Write names of different shapes for which nets are provided.

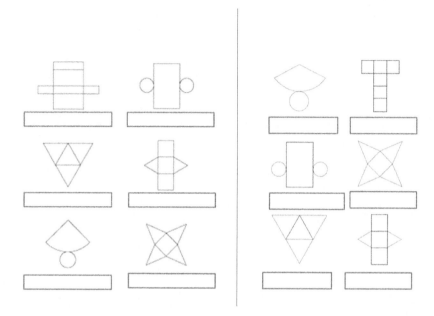

2. Find out a least dividend which can be divided by 20, 30, 50 and 120 exactly leaving a remainder 11 in each case.

3. Three bells ring at an interval of 8 seconds, 12 seconds and 16 seconds respectively. After what time interval do they ring jointly? How many times do they strike jointly within an hour?

[Ans: 48 seconds; 75times]

4. Rashabh painted a box alone in 6 hours; Mohit can paint it alone in 9 hours. Both of them jointly can paint it in ___ hours and____ minutes.

[Ans: 3 hours and 36 minutes]

5. How many diagonals are there in a hexagon?

6. Simplify:

$$\left(1 + \frac{1}{100}\right) X \left(1 - \frac{91}{101}\right) X \left(1 + \frac{1}{1000}\right) X \left(1 - \frac{901}{1001}\right) X \, 1313$$

$$= \underline{\hspace{2cm}} X \, 0.01$$

7. What least number should be subtracted from 101,112 to make the number exactly divisible by 101?

8. A bus started from the Bus Terminus of a city at 7:32 a.m. morning and reached another city 7:51 a.m. the next day. Find the duration of the entire journey.

9. Observe the number pattern and complete the chart given below:

1+ 3   = 4 = 2X2;

1 + 3 + 5 +7   = __ = ____;

1 + 3 + 5 +7 + 9   = __ = ____;

1 + 3 + 5 + 7 + 9 + 11   = __ = ____;

1 + 3 + 5 + 7 + 9 + 11 +13   = __ = ____;

1 + 3 + 5 + 7 + 9 + 11 +13 + 15   = __ = 8 X 8;

10. Roshanlal observed that his sum deposited in a bank amounts to double in ten years. Find the rate percent of the Simple Interest provided by that bank.

[Ans: 10% of Simple Interest per anum]

11. 80% of 240 is how much more than 35% of 400?

12. A seven digit number is represented as follows:

H Th	T Th	Th	H	T	O
3	2	6	8	__	__

Statement: This number is the greatest possible multiple of 8 located in between 326,880 and 326,900. The number is also divisible by 2 and 4. The number is also divisible by 16.

Provide the maximum possible digits at tens and ones place to make the given statement true.

13. A number located in between 24200 and 24400 is a multiple of 121. That number is also divisible by 11 without leaving any remainder. Find the number.

14. A craftsperson earns $ 3.03 per hor. He works 8 hours a day and five days a week. Find his earnings of 5 weeks duration.

15. There is a road outside the semicircular park of specific dimensions as depicted in the figure.

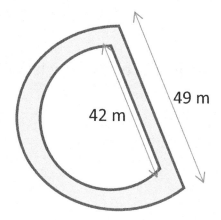

Calculate the fencing of that path from both outer side and inner side.

16. The LCM of 36, 72 and 144 is greater than their HCF by _____.

17. A regular pentagon has _____ rotational symmetry less than those of a regular hexagon.

18. A nursing home can accommodate 120 patients in their general ward and 30 patients in ICU. 70% of all beds were filled up last week. Find the number of beds remained empty last week.

19. Half of a work is done by Rikin in 8 days and quarter of the same work can be finished by Mark alon. In how many days do they jointly finish the complete work?

20. Identify a three digit greatest number which is divisible by 2, 4 and 8 leaving remainder 1 in each case.

21. _____ is the only even prime number.

22. Area of a square shaped crop field is 144 sq. m. Find length of each side of the square field.

Worksheet 13

1. Find the equivalent number in standard form:

$$(2 \times 100) + \left(30\ X\frac{1}{10}\right) + \left(4\ X\ \frac{1}{10}\right) + \left(22\ X\frac{1}{100}\right) + \left(121\ X\frac{1}{1000}\right)$$

2. How many different angles are formed? Write names of each angle.

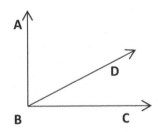

3. If two lines intersect each other at a definite point then how many pairs of vertically opposite angles are formed?

4. Which of the following is not a property of rectangles?

   a. Opposite sides are parallel to each other.
   b. Opposite angles are supplementary to each other.
   c. All the interior angles are right angles.
   d. Pair of diagonals intersects each other at right angle.
   e. Sum total of all the interior angles is equal to two straight angles.
   f. Two greatest possible triangles can be adjusted inside it without overlapping.
   g. It is a special type of parallelogram.
   h. This figure cannot be defined as a square.

5. Mr Ravikumar can paint a wall in 6 days and his counterpart can paint it in 12 days. Both of them jointly can paint it in _____ days.

6. The measure of an angle is 54^0. What is the measure of its complement?

7. Write T for true or F for false for the following statements.

   a. There are eight prime numbers in between 1 and 20.

   b. All prime numbers has only one factor.

   c. All composite numbers has more than two factors.

   d. 69 is a multiple of 1, 3 and 23.

   e. There is only one prime number in between 90 and 100.

   f. Sum total of 21 hundredths and 543 thousandths is greater than 1.

   g. All natural numbers are not composite numbers.

   h. Any number divisible by 5 should have digit 0 or 5 at its one's place.

   i. Any number divisible by 8 is also divisible separately by all the other factors of 8, 4 and 2.

8. Rikin pointed out a mistake in the representation of a greatest five digit number divisible by 11 submitted by his friend Mike and corrected the mistake by reducing the digit at one's place by 4. What was the result submitted by Mike?

9. Ramantha observed that sum total of three consecutive prime number is 15. Sum total of the first and last prime number is half of the second one. Find all the prime numbers.

10. Aman and Natalia went on completing their projects jointly in 16 days. If Aman alone could do it in 32 days then Natalia alone could do it in _____ days.

11. Bishan Singh three cu. m. earth in a day by working 8 hours a day. An assignment was issued to him to dig a chamber of dimension 6 m X 10 m X 10 m by working 10 hours a day at the time of emergency. Bishan Singh could complete his assignment in _____ days.

12. Find the least number which can divide 126, 25,200 and 504,000 exactly without leaving any remainder.

13. Find the least numbers to be subtracted from each of the following numbers to make them all divisible by 11.

    992, 9994, 99999, 9090907, 880,880,880

14. Arrange the following in ascending order:

    20% of 12, 30 % of 32 , one sixth of 18.18, three seventh of 49.49

15. There exists some similarity between regular pentagon and regular hexagon. Identify the point which cannot signify their similarities.

    a. Sum total of all the exterior angles of both the polygon is equal to a complete angle.
    b. Interior angle of the hexagon is 36^0 more than that of the pentagon.

c. Number of diagonals in pentagon is 5 and number such diagonals in hexagon is 9.

d. Three non- overlapping triangles can be accommodated in pentagon and four such triangles can be accommodated in hexagon.

16. Place a suitable digit at the place marked as * to make the given numbers divisible by both 3 and 9.

126*9, 1322*76, 206,54*,121*32

17. Which greatest three digit number is divisible exactly by 4?

18. Roshanlal divided a rectangle in eight equal parts and observed that if such square sized cut pieces are arranged serially side by side then a rectangle of perimeter 36 cm is obtained. Find the dimension of the original rectangle.

19. When 0.02968 is divided by 0.008, what will be the quotient?

20. If we multiply a fraction by itself and divide the product by its reciprocal, the fraction thus obtained is $18\dfrac{26}{27}$. What is the original fraction?

21. A triangle having any two sides equal to each other should have _____ angles equal to each other. The unequal side will be _____ to the unequal angle.

22. Mohanlal painted 1/20th of a wall in 4 days. He will complete his works in _____ days.

23. A flower garden is 22.50 m long. Sheela wants to make a border along one side using bricks that are 0.25 m long. How many bricks will be needed?

24. Ravi can do half of a work alone in 12 days, Munish can do quarter of the same work in 18 days and Roushan can complete one tenth of the work in 2 days. If they all join hands to complete the same work then by what time the entire work will be finished?

Worksheet 14

1. How many six digit numbers are there in all?
2. 1080 more than _____ is 30080.
3. Last two digit of the greatest seven digit even multiple of 3 is ____.
4. _____ must be subtracted from six digit greatest even number to make it a multiple of 4.
5. The greatest seven digit number which is not a multiple of 9, but a multiple of 3 is _____.
6. Which digit should come at the blank space to make the statement true?
7. Digit 7 used _____ times while writing all the numbers starting from 1 to 100.
8. The speed of a car is increased from 60 km/h to 70 km/h. calculate the time saved by the rider while driving through a distance of 420 km.
9. The sum total of 4 consecutive two digit even numbers is 12 more than eight times ten. Find the numbers.
10. Five years ago Nikita reached at her teenage. Five years hence she will be at her _____ years of age.
11. Rishabh paints a wall in 12 days and his counterpart Chelladurai paints it in 16 days. They jointly started working to finish the wall painting in _____days.
12. Anamika measured a length of 1.2 m, 1.6 m and 2.8 m ribbons by using her greatest possible measuring scale. Find the length of her scale.
13. Three bells toll at in intervals of 12 seconds, 16 seconds and 18 seconds respectively. After what interval of time do they toll together?
14. Complete the following:
$$\frac{121}{144}X\frac{12}{169}X\frac{26}{225}X\frac{15}{242}X\frac{15}{77}X\frac{91}{100}X\frac{11}{100}X \text{\_\_\_} = 0.0001$$

15. Sixteen square shaped uniform tiles of side 4 cm each are arranged in two different patterns. In the first pattern tiles are joined to form a largest possible square. In the second pattern tiles are joined side by side to form a longest possible rectangle. Find out the difference in their outer boundaries.

16. Mr Ravikumar observed that the hour hand and minute hand of a wall mount clock makes _____ and _____ complete turns on the dial throughout a day.

17. Vijayan installed two cisterns for filling up the water tank . First cistern alone can fill it in 1 hour 40 minutes and second cistern can fill it in 2 hours 30 minutes. Both the cisterns can fill the water tank in _____ hours ____ minutes.

18. Three interior angles of a triangle are in such a way that sum total of first two angle is equal to the third angle, and first angle is twice the second. Find out all the interior angles.

19. _____ is the greatest possible six digit number divisible by 2, 4 and 8 without leaving remainders.

20. Half of a quarter of six tenths of a number is 120. Find the number.

21. Nikitha travels 360 km on three fifths of the petrol tank of her car. How far would she travel at the same rate with a full tank of petrol of her car?

22. Find which of the statement regarding a parallelogram is not true.

   a. Opposite sides are equal to each other and parallel to each other.
   b. Sum total of all the interior angles is two times greater then a straight angle.
   c. Diagonals bisect the figure into two congruent triangles.

d. Two diagonals are not equal to each other.

e. It can represent most of the properties of a rhombus excluding the properties of the diagonals. That means rhombus is a special type of parallelogram in which sides are equal to each other.

Worksheet 15

1. The table below shows the water used by a family having 5 members.

Activity	Water in Litres(l)
a. Cooking and drinking	30 l
b. Washing	105 l
c. Cleaning pots, pans	40 l
d. Bathing	120 l
e. Gardening	85 l

Total water used by them _____

i.   Find the average per head consumption of water.

ii.   Which activity requires least amount of water?

2. A wall mount clock strikes three bells in three seconds at 3 O' Clock. Find the time taken by that clock to strike 10 bells at 10 P.M.

3. Mr Ravikumar checked his mobile at 9 a.m. and found that it is showing a time which is _____ hours more than the GMT. The place whete Mr Ravikumar residing is at 90^0 East to the GMT time zone. Time increases at the rate of 4 minutes per one degree change in the meridian towards eastern direction. What was the GMT ?

4. Pressure of a gas increases when volume is decreased. The product of pressure and volume of certain mass of gas always remains constant. The volume will be decreased by _____ fraction when pressure of the gas is doubled.

5. Which number is equal to the difference of fifth multiple of 20 and fifteenth multiple of 3?

6. Complete the following expansion:

$$102.2032 = 100 + \underline{\quad} + \frac{2}{10} + \frac{\quad}{100} + \frac{\quad}{1,000} + \frac{2}{10,000}$$

7. Find the value :

$$\left(\frac{1}{2}X\frac{2}{3}X\frac{3}{4}X\text{.......}X\frac{999999}{1,000,000}\right)X\ 11,00011 =$$

8. Which number comes at the fifth step if we continue multiplying 1.10011 repeatedly by 10?

9. Rajan completes his assignment in 12 days and Nikitha completes the same assignment alone in 16 days. If they work jointly upon the same assignment, then in how many days do they complete the same assignment?

10. The minute hand of a clock makes 360^0 at the dial during a complete rotation. Find the angle made by the minute hand at the dial during a day.

11. Rishabh observed that if we multiply 15 to a number then it becomes 60 times greater than 4. Find the original number.

12. Namitha made a decimal representation in such a way that the number was a least value of 5 digits without repeating any digit twice. Also the number had five places of decimals. Find the product of digits at thousandths and ten thousandths place.

13. By heating 100 kg sandstone 44 kg carbon dioxide is obtained. Calculate the mass of sandstone required for obtaining 8.8 kg carbon dioxide.

14. Arrange the following in ascending order:

    12%, 1.2, 12 tenths, 12 thousandths, 12 tens, 12 hundredths, (12 X 0.101)

15. Is there any prime number located in between 80 and 90? If yes, then find their sum total.

16. Cost of 3 pencils and 4 pens is ₹ 77. Total cost of 4 pencils and 3 pens is ₹ 63. Find the total cost of 10 pens and 11 pencils.

17. Monika prepared a chart to show two different closed figures each of which are made of 81 identical square sized silver papers in such a way that one of the shapes has maximum possible outer boundary and the other shape has least outer boundary. If the area of each silver paper is 1 sq. inch, then find the dimensions of both the shapes made by Monika.

18. What least number must be added to the smallest six digit number to make it a multiple of 9?

19. Find the values of the following:

a) 11 tens + 11 tenths + 11 hundredths + 11 thousandths

b) $\dfrac{11}{100} + \dfrac{101}{1000} + \dfrac{1001}{1000} + \dfrac{10001}{10000} + 101$

c) $\left(1 + \dfrac{1}{10}\right) X \left(1 + \dfrac{1}{11}\right) X \dots \left(1 + \dfrac{1}{999}\right) =$

d) $5 - 5 + 5 - 5 + 5 - 5 + \dots \; 170 \; times =$

e) $\left(1 + \dfrac{1}{1 - \dfrac{1}{1 + \dfrac{1}{10}}}\right) =$

20. Pamela calculated the sum total of all the prime number located in between 1 and 22 and found that her result was 21 less than the original result. Which of the two prime numbers were missing in her sum total chart?

21. Fractions obtained on multiplying or dividing both numerator and denominator of a given fraction by the same non-zero number, and the given fraction are called _____ fractions.

22. Half of a loin cloth is used for making napkins, quarter of the rest of the cloth is used for making duster, one nineth of the rest of the cloth is used for designing a curtain. Cloth remained after all the above activities is 29.29 cm. find the total length of the loin cloth.

23. A drum contains 20 litres of a paint. From this, 2 litres of paint is taken out and replaced by 2 litres of oil. Again 2 litres of this mixture is taken out and replaced by 2 litres of oil. If this operation is performed once again, then what would be the final ratio of paint and oil in the drum ?

Worksheet 16

1. Roderick took a car for reaching his office in time. The car was moving with an average speed. It took 4 hours to reach his office which is 240 km away from his house. The car was moving through the second lane of express way having a speed limit of 60 km/h. The speed limit of first lane of that express way is 80 km/h. find the total time which could be saved by Roderick if he prefers moving through the first lane instead of the second.

2. 20 % of a number is 8 more than the 8th multiple of 100. Find the original number.

3. Find the value:

$$\frac{11}{100} + \frac{11}{1000} + \frac{11}{10000} + 0.101 + 1.01 =$$

4. What least number must be subtracted from 121019.049 to make this value exactly divisible by 8 without extending the place of decimals beyond hundredths?

5. The average of six person's age is 12 years. After joining a senior person the average is increased by 3 years 2 months. Find age of the senior.

6. A number is increased by 6.6 to make it a five digit smallest natural number exactly divisible by 11. Find the original number.

7. Donadoni is 4 years older than Mike, who is again 3.5 years younger than Rick. Rick will enter his teenage after 3 years. Find the age of all the fellows.

8. Add the following:

40% of 64 + 25% of 81 + 50% of 125

9. Subtract 14 thousandths from 14 tenths and multiply the result by 5 hundredths.

10. Richardson throws a baseball at a speed of 72 km/h and his counterpart Ambarish throws it at an average speed of 20 m/s. who throws the ball at a greater speed?

11. Add the following fractions:

$$6\frac{2}{11} + 5\frac{3}{33} + 4\frac{5}{55} + 3\frac{1}{22}$$

12. First angle of a scalene triangle is two times of the second angle and half of the third angle. Find all the three angles.

13. Simplify the following:

8 + {22 X [15 + (14 X 2)]}

14. Which decimal is equivalent to the following expression?

$$\frac{101}{1000} X \frac{11}{100} X \frac{1}{10} X \frac{1}{100} X 3,000$$

15. A cistern can fill up an empty tank of water in 45 minutes, while another cistern will take 1 hour 30 minutes to fill up the same tank. Find the time taken by both the tank to fill up the same empty water tank.

16. Which least number should be subtracted from a four digit greatest number to make the number divisible by 8?

Worksheet 17

1. Area of a square is 64 square cm. Its outer boundary = _____ cm.

2. The factors of 36 are: 1 and _____, 2 and _____, 4 and _____, _____ and 12, _____ and 6

3. Your brother needs help baking brownies for the school bake sale.

4. One recipe he has calls for eight eggs. Remove eight eggs from the carton below.

5. To show you have removed eggs color them red. Shade in the remaining eggs yellow.

   a. What fraction of the entire set is 8 eggs? _____

   b. Write an equivalent fraction for the amount in question 1.

   c. How many eggs still remain?

6. 4. What fraction of the set still remains?

7. _____

8. 5. Write an equivalent fraction for the amount in question 4.

   _____

9. 6. Write a fraction sentence to show how many eggs were removed and how many still remain.

10. What least number must be added to 121112X 0.001 to make it a multiple of 1.001?

11. A wall mount clock takes 4 seconds for striking 4 bells it will take _____ seconds for striking 10 bells at 10 O'Clock.

[Ans: 12 Seconds]

Standard Form	Expanded Form
1020.3257	1 X 1000 + 2 X 10 + $\dfrac{3}{10} + \dfrac{2}{100} + \dfrac{5}{1000} + \dfrac{7}{10000}$
304.9081	
2040.5908	

12. Wheel of a car rotates three times for crossing a distance equal to 1.25 m. Find the total rotation made by that wheel for crossing a distance of 6 km 250 m.

13. Complete the chart:

14. Angles of a quadrilateral are in the ratio of 6:3:4:5. Find the measures of all the interior angles of this quadrilateral.

15.   Athlete Niharika runs five times around a square field to cover a distance equal to 2 km. Find the area of the field. Also find the cost of renovating the field at the rate of Rs 50 per square metre.

16.   Mr Nandanwar covers half of his entire journey by train, half of the rest of the journey by bus, half of the remaining distance by car and rest of the 5.05 km by auto. Find the distance of the entire journey covered by him.

17.   Simplify:

$$\frac{12}{169} X \frac{13}{144} X \left(1 + \frac{1}{23}\right)\left(1 + \frac{1}{25}\right)\left(1 + \frac{2}{50}\right)\left(1 + \frac{1}{4}\right) =$$

{ Ans : 0.008]

Worksheet 18

1. First tap can fill a water tank in 45 minutes and second tap can empty the half filled tank in 1.5 hours. By what time the empty tank will be filled up if both the taps kept open?

2. Half of a cake is given to all friends, half of the remaining portion of the cake retained by parents, one third of what remaining was distributed amongst John's classmates. Finally John received only 200 g of the cake. Find the quantity of that cake.

3. Complete the number series:
   a. 1.1.2.3.5.____,____, _____.

4. $\frac{1}{3}, \frac{3}{5}, \frac{5}{7},$ ....   Ratio of 10th and 15th value = _____.

5. Josephine is on an 1,800 calorie per day diet. She tries to keep her intake of fat to no more than 30% of her total calories. Based on an 1,800 calorie a day diet, what is the maximum number of calories that Josephine should consume from fats per day to stay within her goal?

6. 125 is what percentage of 625 ?

7. Nikita deposited a sum in a bank with a condition of withdrawing 4/5th of the amount after a span of 6 years. Any deposit in that bank becomes 8/5th of the principal in 5 years. After withdrawing such amount after the tenure the amount left in that bank was Rs 1750. Find the percentage of simple interest and the principal that Nikita deposited in the Bank.

8. Rainfall of a state in the month of July was recorded 125 mm. It was also equal to 15% of rainfall of that state of the year. Find the annual rainfall of that state.

9. Mohan measured a distance of 306 km by using his measuring tape having a length of 800 m. how many times that tape was used completely. What fraction of that tap was used during the last time?

10. What least number must be subtracted from a greatest five digit even number to make it divisible by 8? Is this number also divisible by 12?

11. Sum total of digits of ones and hundreds place is equal to the digit located at tens place. Number formed by last two digits is a greatest possible multiple of 4. Find the reciprocal of that number.

12. Municipal Corporation of a city has decided to organize plantation works beside a 25 km long road by placing trees beside both the sides of the road at an interval of 50 m. find the total number of trees that can be planted. Also find the cost of maintaining those plants at a rate of $ 2 for every 5 plants.

13. Selling price of an item is 1/15th more than the Cost Price. Find the percentage of profit.

14. Cost of 4 pens and 5 pencils is $ 25. The cost of 7 pens and 6 pencils is $ 41. Find the cost of a set of 10 pens and 10 pencils. At the same rate the ratio of the cost of a pen and a pencil is _____.

15. A rectangular vegetable garden of dimension 40m X 30m was fenced leaving two gates of 3m each on both the side at the rate of $2 per m. Find the percentage of the garden which was fenced. Also find the cost of fencing.

16. Fractions like ½, 1/3, ¼, 1/8, 1/12, are also called _____ fractions.

17. Five tenths is _____ times greater that five hundredths and _____ times smaller than 5.

18. Four electric lights are turned on at the same time. First one blinks every 4 seconds, second one blinks every 6 seconds, third one blinks every 8 seconds and the fourth one blinks every 12 seconds. In 60 seconds, how many times will they blink at the same time?

19. Find the greatest six digit number which is exactly divisible by 4 but not divisible by 8.

20. Reciprocal of 0.125 and 0.0625 are arranged side by side to make a natural number. Find the difference of the greatest and smallest such numbers.

[Hints: Since $0.75 = \dfrac{75}{100} = \dfrac{3}{4}$, therefore reciprocal of 0.75 will be $\dfrac{100}{75} = \dfrac{4}{3}$. In the similar way reciprocals of 0.125 and 0.0625 can be worked out.]

21. In a busy airport, aeroplanes from New Delhi Airport depart every 60 minutes whilst aeroplanes from Bangalore Airport depart every 90 minutes. If both airports have aeroplanes departing at 15:45 Hours when is the next time they will depart from the airport together again?

22. Observe the given figure and answer the questions as follows.

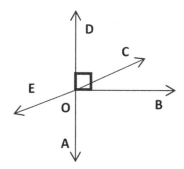

a. How many acute angles are there?

b. < AOB = _____.

c. < AOD = _____.

d. Which angle is supplementary to <AOC?

e. Which angle is complementary to <BOC?

f. How many obtuse angles can be named?

g. Reflex angle of <AOE.

Worksheet 19

1. Which prime number is greater than 90 but smaller than 100?

2. Name all the angles represented in the given figure.

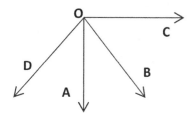

3. If we multiply a two digit greatest possible number by 4 then it becomes a multiple of 8. Find such greatest possible number which can be obtained by subtracting _____ from the two digit greatest number.

4. Find the area of the portion enclosed by both the outer boundaries of concentric circles.

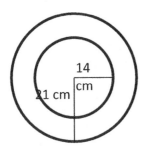

5. Pencils come in packages of 20. Erasers come in packages of 24. Lara wants to purchase the smallest number of pencils and erasers in such a way that she will have exactly 1 eraser per pencil. How many packages of pencils and erasers should Lara buy?

6. Tours for the National Museum leave every 15 minutes. Tours for the Zoo leave every 20 minutes. Tours for the Red Fort leaves every 10 minutes. How often do the tours leave at the same time?

7. Half of the half of the successor of a three digit greatest number is _____ less than the two digit greatest number.

8. A wall mount clock takes 2 seconds for striking 2 bells at 2 O'clock. Calculate the time taken by that clock to strike 10 bells at 10 O'clock.

9. A 200 m long train takes 30 seconds to cross a telephone post. Calculate the time taken by the same train with same speed to cross a 900m long platform.

10. What least number must be added to the smallest seven digit number to make it exactly divisible by 11?

11. Measure of an interior angle of a regular pentagon is _____ less than that of a regular heptagon.

12. After reaching home at 10:30 am Mohini observed that her wall mount clock was running 23 minutes 23 seconds late. She wanted to attend her dance class after

55 minutes. By what time in accord to her clock she should prepare herself for the same?

13. Ravi can do a piece of work in 10 days and Nitin can do the same work in 20 days. By what time do they jointly can finish the work?

14. Sum total of two interior angles of a triangle is 1210. Find reflex angle of the third angle.

15. What least number must be added to a seven digit even number to make it divisible by both 4 and 8?

16. Every 2nd, 5th and 10th visitor of a shopping complex receives gifts. How often do three visitors at a time will receive gifts?

17. Six consecutive numbers are in such a way that product of the greatest and smallest number is equal to 72. Find the ratio of third and fifth such numbers.

18. A regular polygon has an exterior angle which is four times smaller than the interior angle. Find the number of sides that the polygon has.

19. What percentage of 625 exceeds 100 by one fourth of a hundred?

20. Nitin started running through a half circle track of diameter 85 m and completed the track 5 times. Find the total distance covered by him.

21. Is there a pair of numbers having HCF 16 and LCM 121?

22. Tap A can fill a water tank in 20 minutes and tap B can finish the tank in 30 minutes. If both the tap kept open then the tank will be filled in _____ minutes.

23. Stamp collection of Nancy increases at a rate of 10 stamps per month. She started stamp collection in February. She had 210 stamps by the end of July. She had _____ stamps in the month of March.

24. Write names of five different angles from the given figures.

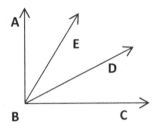

25. Simplify : 36.907 - [19.7 - {14.6 - (15.8 − 4 ÷ 2 x 2)}]

Worksheet 20

1. Complementary of one angle is 2/3rd of the other. Find ratio of their reflex angles.

2. Half of a circle is shaded red, half of the rest of the circle shaded blue, three fourth of the remaining circle shaded green and rest of the part of the circle is divided into three equal parts for putting pink, yellow and purple bands. Find the ratio of all the colours displayed in the circle. If the radius of the circle is 14 cm then find the total area of the pink and purple colours displayed in the circle.

3. Name at least four angles from the given figure.

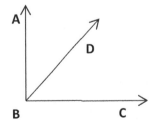

4. Mohini used 2/3rd of the water present in a half filled can. After using water the empty portion of the can was equal to 254 ml. Find the total capacity of the can.

5. Rohan and Rohini went on measuring the play ground of dimension 31.5m X 46.5 m by using a longest possible stick which can be used for a multiple times without leaving any portion off the measurement. Find the length of that stick.

6. Pencils come in packages of 20. Erasers come in packages of 24. Lara wants to purchase the smallest number of pencils and erasers in such a way that she will have exactly 1 eraser per pencil. How many packages of pencils and erasers should Lara buy?

7. Two concentric circular discs used to make a design. Difference of their radii is 7 cm and difference of their outer boundaries is 44 cm. Find the area of the space bounded by both the linings of these circular discs.

8. Find the temperature at which the reading of Celsius scale will be 2/5th of that of Fahrenheit scale.

9. $\left(1 - \dfrac{1}{10}\right)\left(1 - \dfrac{1}{11}\right)...\left(1 - \dfrac{1}{1000}\right) = \ ?$

10. After increasing the selling price of an item by $ 100 a shopkeeper gains 10% profit instead of a 10% loss. Find the original cost price of that item.

11. Earning of Mahesh is equal to 4/5th of that of Rina and 11/13th of that of Kamalika. Find the ratio of their earnings.

12. What percentage of 144 exceeds 25 by 3.8?

13. Simplify: 27.9 - [3.08 - {4.6 - (1.5 – 1.3 - 2)}]

14. Quarter of a water tank is equal to the one sixth of another tank. Both the tanks can jointly hold 1,200 litres of water. Find the capacity of both the tank.

15. Three bells toll at an interval of 5 minutes, 8 minutes and 12 minutes respectively. They toll together at 17:46 Hrs. when do they toll together again?

16. Total cost of 3 pens and 2 pencils is $20, again total cost of 4 pens and 6 pencils $36. What will be the total cost of 7 pens and 11 pencils?

17. Two angles of a right triangle are in the ratio of 2.3. Find the angles.

18. Simplify:

$$14\frac{1}{20} \times 4 \times 5\frac{7}{10} \times 10\frac{13}{20} \times \frac{1}{57} \times \frac{11}{213} \times \frac{3}{281}$$

19. Find the ratio of reflex angle of 39^0, complementary of 19^0 and supplementary of 39^0.

20. Angle p forms a linear pair with angle q. angle r forms a linear pair with angle s. ratio of p and q is 4:5 and that of r and s is 11:7. Find the ratio of four given angles a, b c and d.

21. Solve the following:

$$3 \div 16 + 1.2 \times \frac{1}{4} - \{\frac{1}{5} + (1 - 0.8)\}$$

Worksheet 21

1. ____ % of 0.5 = 0.005

2. A recipe calls for two-thirds of a cup of sugar. You find that you only have one-half of a cup of sugar left.

3. The area of a rectangular floor that is fourteen and one-half feet wide is two hundred thirty-nine and one-fourth square feet. Find the perimeter of the floor.

4. Complete the following:

$$\frac{3}{5} = \frac{6}{-} = \frac{15}{-} = \frac{}{60} = \frac{}{150}$$

5. Rohit can finish one third of a work in 6 days and Mohit can finish one sixth of the same work in 3 days. Both of the jointly can finish the same work in _____ days.

6. A package of 40 miniature Choco bars contains a total of 700 calories. Each candy bar contains the same food value. How many calories does 12 candy bar contain? How many candy bars can replace 25 Choco bars?

7. Rani visits her local hardware shop and sees that there is 50% off a kitchen whose list price is $ 5000.   Two days later the same kitchen has a sign on it "Further reduction of 20% on last week's price". She visits the shop again at the weekend and sees that there is a new sign on the kitchen "Weekend special – further reduction of 10%". She decides to buy - what will she pay?
   a. Rani bought the kitchen which originally cost $5000 for $1800. How much did she save?
      i. What fraction of the original price was this?
      ii. What % of the original price was this?
      iii. If you were the shopkeeper would you tell your customers 50%, then 20%, then 10% or just say " _____ % off"?

8. In a survey of 22,000 people, 14,300 responded that watching T.V. was the most important consideration in their daily life. What percent of the people felt that watching T.V. was not the most important consideration?

9. Find three prime numbers between 60 and 80. Also find their sum total.

10. Simplify: 23.09 - [21.7 - {20.8 - (46.6 – 23.5 – 23.4)}]

11. Forty-nine percent of all people who buy sporting shoes don't run at all. Assuming 680,000 people buy sporting shoes, how many will use them to run in?

12. ___% of _50_ % of 72 = 9.

13. A square shaped rod having sides of one tenth of a meter is used for making a circular ring. Find the circumference of the ring. Also find the distance covered by that ring in 360 complete spins.

14. ___ is the smallest positive whole number and ___ is the largest negative whole number.

15. 5+ (-5)+ 5+ (-5)+ ____ 5+ (-5)   169 times = _____.

16. Edwin makes a 12% down payment on a home in Paris. What was the purchase price of the home if his down payment is $35,200?

17. Half a score banana costs $ 6. Find the cost of six dozen bananas.

18. Four bells toll at an interval of 5, 12, 18 and 24 minutes respectively. If they toll together at 11:30 am, then when do they toll together again?

19. A regular polygon has an exterior angle which is four times smaller than the interior angle. Find the number of sides that the polygon has.

20. What fraction of a number is 15% of its original value?

21. _____ is a solid three dimensional shape having no vertices. It has only one curved face.

22. 20 % of 20 % of 400 = _____ % of 320.

23. Robert can finish one tenth of a work in ten days. His another associate Bill can finish two fifteenth of the same work in ten days. If they work together then they can finish the same work in _____ days.

24. 1 + 2 + 3 + ------ + 100 = _____
    a. =   (100+1) + (99 +2) + ---- + (50 +51)
    b. =   101+101+----- 50 times   =   101X50   =   5050
    c. Similarly find …
    d. 1+ 2 + 3+ ------ + 1000 = _____
    e. 1 + 2 + 3 + …. + 10,000 = _____.
    f. 4 + 8 + 12 + …. 4.000 = _____.

25. Simplify:

45.08 - [38.12 - {60.9 ÷ 3 – (16.6 – 11.9 ÷ 3.8) ÷ 3}]

26. Observe the number pattern …

1, 1, 2, 3, 5, _, 13, 21, ____, _____

    a. Provide missing numbers.

    b. Provide seventh number of the series.

    c. Sum total of fourth and sixth value =

    d. What is the nature of progress?

27. 13 million + 324 thousand + 3024 hundred = _____.

Worksheet 22

1. A wall mount clock sreikes 4 bells at 4 p.m. in 4 seconds. Find the time taken by that clock to strike 11 bells at 11 p.m.

2. Nithin got Rs. 124 as an interest form a bank for his deposit of certain amount for the period of 2 years. Find the principal amount.

3. Mohan is 4 times older than his sister Mohini. Before a couple of years he was five times older than Mohini. Find their ages after ten years.

4. $\dfrac{5}{6}, \dfrac{5}{8}, \dfrac{5}{11}, \dfrac{5}{13}$ are examples of _____ fractions having identical numerators.

5. 12% of 29 = 14% 0f _____.

6. Mohini deposited a sum of money in a bank and received a simple interest of Rs 1250 after five years of time period at a rate of 6.5% per annum. Find the amount that she can receive on the same principal after 10 years.

7. A number having only two factors is a _____.

8. All _____ numbers have more than ___ factors. All such factors are _____ than or equal to the number.

9. John makes and sells juice drinks. The juice drinks are sold in six-packs and boxes. A six-pack has 6 juice drinks and costs $2.

10. 4, 14, 10, 28 These are all multiples of: _____.

11. There are _____ prime factors in 507.

12. The grocer at a shop arranged 10 rows of cans. There were 2 cans in the first row, 4 cans in the second row, and 6 cans in the third row. The grocer continued to add 2 cans to each new row.
    a. How many cans did the grocer put in the fifth row? Show or explain how you got   your answer.

    b. What is the total number of cans the grocer arranged in all 10 of the rows? Show or explain how you got your answer.

    c. Describe the relationship between the row number and the number of cans in each row.

13. Determine the sum of the measures of the exterior angles of following regular polygons.
    a. Hexagon   b. Octagon   c. 23-sided polygon   d. 100-sided polygon

14. Nine times of a number added to ten thousand is 10,999. Find the number.

15. Fraction of "M" in the word "MATHEMATICS" = __

16. One fifth of 3 score is _____% of 500.

17. Rosi is walking around the outside of a building that is in the shape of a regular polygon. She determines that the measure of one exterior angle of the building is 30°. Find the number of sides that the outer lining of the building have.

18. Complete the following table to display the relationship of number of sides of a regular polygon with its measure of interior angles.

a. an Interior angle	No. of sides
b. 120°	_____
c. 72°	_____
d. 135°	_____
e. 90°	4
f. 60°	_____

19. A wall mount clock takes 8 seconds for striking 3 bells. Calculate the time taken by the same clock for striking ...
   a. 6 bells   b. 8 bells   c. 10 bells

20. Complementary angle of a supplementary angle of angle P is 43⁰ . Find the sum total of both complementary and supplementary angles of angle P.

21. A right triangle has other two angles in the ratio of 4:1. Find the magnitude of both the angles.

22. Dr Sarkar reached his chamber 5 minutes late, but the wall mount clock was displaying a time to show that he has reached his chamber 12 minutes before. The wall mount clock of the chamber is running fast by _____ minutes. Actual time when Dr Sarkar reached his chamber was _____.

23. Observe the figure and answer the questions as follows.

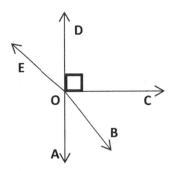

a. Complementary of <AOB = _____.

b. A Straight angle. _____.

c. Supplement of <EOD = _____.

d. A Linear pair: _____ and _____.

e. A perpendicular upon line AD. _____.

Worksheet 23

Fill in the blanks:

(i) 79, 83 and 97 are _____ numbers.

(ii) The smallest composite number of three digits exactly divisible by 3 and 9 is

_____.

(iii) The smallest natural number exactly divisible by 111, 3 and 9 is _____.

(iv) The smallest positive whole number exactly divisible by 11 and 3 is _____.

(v) The first 3 multiples of 12 are _____.

(vi) 3, 7, 9, 15, 25 are _____ numbers.

(vii) _____ is a factor of every number.

(viii) _____ is a factor of every even number. Every even number is a multiple of

_____.

(ix) 2, 3, 5 and 7 are prime numbers. A _____ number has only 2 factors one and the

number itself.

(x) A composite number has more than _____ factors.

(xi) The factors of 16 are _____.

(xii) A number is a factor of another number if on dividing the _____ is zero.

(xiii) 121, 484 and 1331 are related in terms of their divisibility. All the three numbers

are exactly divisible by a greatest possible common factor. Such common factor is

_____.

2. Find the digit present in the thousands place in the product

(11011÷ 11) X 7000 = _____

3. Mandela wanted to add three digit greatest number to another number to obtain a

five digit smallest number. He has added _____ to the third multiple of 333.

4. At 3 O Clock and 9 O Click both hour hand and minute hand of a clock makes an angle

of ___a_____ which is __b__ of a complete angle.

A: a= 90^0 b = $1/4^{th}$

B: a= 180^0 b = $1/2^{nd}$

C: a= 270^0 b = $1/3^{rd}$

D: a= 30^0 b = $1/12^{th}$

5. One fourth of a scale is equal to one tenth of another scale. For measuring a ribbon of 8m the longer scale is used ten times. Find the length of the shorter scale.

A: 1 m   B: 2 m

C: 3 m   D: 4 m

6. The floor of a room a hotel is 12 m long and 10 m wide. 45 tiles of 1 m square was in stock. Tiles come in market in pack of ten tiles. How many more 1m square tiles does the manager need to completely cover the floors of three such rooms?

I: 15 tiles more than 30 full pack

II: 5 tiles more than 31 full pack

III: 25 tiles more than 29 full pack

IV: 50 tiles more than 25 full pack

Select your answers

A: Only I   B: Only II   C: I, II and III   D: Only IV

7. A regular pentagon has __a___ lines of symmetry less than a hexagon. It has _____b _____ lines of symmetry more than an equilateral triangle. Both square and equilateral triangle has __ c__ lines of symmetry in all.

	a	b	c
A:	1	2	7
B:	2	4	8
C:	1	2	3
D:	2	4	6

8. Complete the expansion in Indo-Arabic Numeration

a. 98,76,54,321 = 90,00,00,000 + 8,00,00,000 + _____ + 6,00,000

      + 50,000 + _____ + 300 + 20 + 1

b. 32,54,03,320 =

c. 32,43,54,576 =

d. 20,30,40,506 =

e. 78,98,70,670 =

9. A square shaped rod having sides of one tenth of a meter is used for making a circular ring. Find the circumference of the ring. Also find the distance covered by that ring in 360 complete spins.

10. 5+ (-5)+ 5+ (-5)+ _____ 5+ (-5)   169 times = _____.

11. Rohit can finish one third of a work in 6 days and Mohit can finish one sixth of the same work in 3 days. Both of the jointly can finish the same work in _____ days.

12. Malavika used 1/5th of her painting colours for finishing a poster. Another 2/3rd of her painting colours were used to finish wall magazine. The remaining colours left with her was 125 ml. find the total volume of poster colours she had at the beginning.

13. 28, 42, 196, 126 These are all multiples of: _____

14. Four bells toll at an interval of 5, 12, 18 and 24 minutes respectively. If they toll together at 11:30 am, then when do they toll together again?

15. One third of one third of the six digit greatest number is a multiple of a smallest prime number _____. It has other primes such as _____.

16. _____ is a solid three dimensional shape having no vertices. It has only one curved face.

17. 20 % of 20 % of 400 = _____ % of 320.

18. Simplify:

$$\left(1 - \frac{1}{10 + \dfrac{1}{10}}\right) + \frac{11}{19} + 17\frac{7}{38} + 23\frac{3}{38} =$$

19. A plant grows at a rate of certain fixed rate per week and attained a height of 208 cm in a year. Finds its regular rate of growth.

20. Half of a quarter of a number is equal to 101.101. Find the number.

Worksheet 24

1. Two objects at average speed of 60 km/h and 72 km/h are moving in a same direction. The gap between them at initial was 72 km. The faster object was following the slower one. It will cross the slower object after ____ hours and gain an advantage of 224 km after ____ hours.

2. Nitin gained 10% by selling a bat to Harish. Harish again sold it to Munish at a gain of 8%. If Munish paid Rs 654 for the bat, find its original price.

3. By what percentage the greatest three digit number should be reduced to make it divisible by 8?

4. A stack of bricks has two horizontal columns and three vertical rows. 12 more bricks can be adjusted to make it a complete cuboidal stack. Find the numbers of bricks present in the stack.

5. What least number must be subtracted from the greatest seven digit numbers to make it a multiple of 8?

6. A divisor divides 268 ,2488, 148, 124, and 1204 exactly leaving remainder 4 in each case. Find reciprocal of the divisor in the decimal form.

7. The cost of fencing a square shaped garden of side 650 m at the rate of $1.25/m = _____

8. Fill in the blanks:
   a. Brick is a model of _____.
   b. Cuboid is a _____ dimension shape.
   c. The dimensions of a cuboid are _____, _____ and _____ .
   d. Number of faces in cuboid are _____
   e. Number of edges in cuboid are _____
   f. Number of corners in cuboid are _____
   g. Is any face of cuboid a Square? _____
   h. The faces of cuboid are in _____ shape.

9. Complete the following:
   a. 4200 m = _____ km
   b. 1000 d m = ___ km
   c. ½ km = _____ m

d. 1500 da m = _____ km

e. 3000 m = _____ d m

f. 2100 m = _____ da m

10. A 132 m long train takes 20 seconds to cross a light post. Find its average speed in km/h. If the same train moves continuously for 45 minutes then the distance covered by it will be .... Km.

11. Fractions like $\dfrac{1}{2}, \dfrac{1}{4}, \dfrac{1}{7}, \dfrac{1}{11}$ are also called _____ fractions.

12. Four electric lights are turned on at the same time. First one blinks every 4 seconds, second one blinks every 6 seconds, third one blinks every 8 seconds and the fourth one blinks every 12 seconds. In 60 seconds, how many times will they blink at the same time?

13. Every 2nd, 5th and 10th visitor of a shopping complex receives gifts. How often do three visitors at a time will receive gifts?

14. Pencils come in packages of 20. Erasers come in packages of 24. Lara wants to purchase the smallest number of pencils and erasers in such a way that she will have exactly 1 eraser per pencil. How many packages of pencils and erasers should Lara buy?

15. Maria has swimming lessons every fifth day, dance classes every sixth day and painting lessons every third day. If she had a swimming lesson, dance classes and a painting lesson on May 28th, when will be the next date on which she has painting, swimming and dance classes?

16. Six families went to the zoo. Each family has 2 adults and 2 children. The entry fee for each child ticket costs $5.00. An adult ticket costs $9.00. Calculate the total amount that all the six families should pay. Also calculate the amount payable by a couple of such families.

17. $-\dfrac{5}{6}, \dfrac{5}{8}, \dfrac{5}{11}, \dfrac{5}{13}$ are examples of _____ fractions having identical numerators.

18. What percent of 12 is one fifteenth?

19. Is there any fraction having zero as a denominator or zero as a numerator?

20. Rosi is walking around the outside of a building that is in the shape of a regular polygon. She determines that the measure of one exterior angle of the building is 30°. Find the number of sides that the outer lining of the building have.

21. Write names of all the angles formed in the following figure.

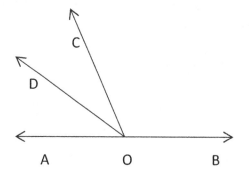 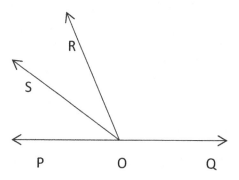

22. Half of a quarter of 720 is _____ less than 100.

Worksheet 25

1. The measure of an interior angle of a regular polygon is given below. How many sides do these polygons have?

an Interior angle	No. of sides
a. 120°	_____
b. 72°	_____
c. 135°	_____

2. You are visiting a friend and their dog gets loose. You chase the dog to try and catch it. You chase it 2 blocks east; it turns and goes 5 blocks west, then 8 blocks east, then another 2 blocks east, 7 blocks west and 1 block east before you finally catch the dog. Use positive numbers to represent east blocks, and negative numbers to represent west blocks. How far are you from your friend's house when you catch the dog?

3. Your school is having an open house. They decide to make bumper stickers with the school logo. The school budgeted $220 for the stickers. It costs $40 to make the design and another $2 for each sticker. How many stickers can the school buy?

4. He must wait until the ground reaches a temperature of 6 degrees Celsius before he can begin building. Jimmy knows that, on average, the temperature increases 2 degrees Celsius per week in the spring. If the temperature is -12 now, how long must Jimmy wait before he can begin work?

5. Marie is buying light bulbs for her Christmas decorations. She buys 12 but when she gets to the cash, she has to put back four because they are broken. How many light bulbs does Marie buy?

6. The lengths of two sides of a triangle are 7 and 11. The third side represented by x. The possible range of x will be : _____ _____

7. Complete: $-\dfrac{11}{24} = \dfrac{...}{48} = \dfrac{......}{72} =$

8. The chart below shows the number of vehicles parked at the beach parking lot on 4 consecutive dates. On July 5th there is a drop of 37% of the total vehicles parked for all four of the previous days. How many vehicles will be parked on the 5th of July? Vehicles parked on 6th of July was seven tenths of total vehicles parked in 2nd July. Find the number of vehicles parked on 6th July.

Date (July)	Number of Cars Parked
1	300
2	400
3	540
4	670
5	654

9. Is there a pair of numbers having HCF 18 and LCM 225?

10. Find the area of the portion enclosed by boundaries of two concentric circles of radii 28 cm and 35 cm respectively.

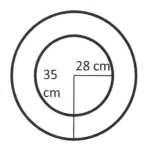

11. In a survey of 22,000 people, 14,300 responded that watching T.V. was the most important consideration in their daily life. What percent of the people felt that watching T.V. was not the most important consideration?

12. What least number must be added to the 7 digit greatest number to make it divisible by 11?

13. A shopkeeper issued three consecutive discounts of 10% on certain purchase. Find the single equivalent discount.

14. What least number must be added to the sex digit greatest number to make it divisible by 8?

15. Cost of a pen and a pencil is $ 6. Cost of 3 pens and 5 pencils is $ 22. Find the cost of 5 pens and 7 pencils. Also find the cost of a pencil.

16. Complete the following:
   a. A number that consists of a whole number and a fraction is called a/an _____ ?
   b. An_____ is a number that represents a part of a whole.
   c. A fraction whose numerical (abrolute) value is greater than 1 is called a/an _____,
   d. and a fraction whose numerical value is between 0 and 1 is called a/an _____
   e. _____ mean the same value.

17. Two sides of a triangle are 6 cm and 13 cm. The length of the third side must be in between _____ cm and _____ cm.

18. 50% of 4.004 is equal to p. Find the value of (p+1)(p - 1) +4pq + 5.

19. Simplify:

$$\left(1 + \frac{1}{10}\right)\left(1 + \frac{1}{100}\right) X\frac{1}{101} X\frac{11}{121} X \left(100 + \frac{1}{10}\right) X\frac{1}{1001}$$

20. Find the greatest five digit number divisible by 8.

2. Assignments

Assignment I

Given below is the number of people who came to watch the soccer matches at the Saltlake stadium during last week of the Premier League Tournament. Observe the data as provided and answer the following questions.

Days	Numbers of Spectators
Monday	24,087
Tuesday	19,701
Wednesday	18,240
Thursday	23,674
Friday	26,326
Saturday	29,530
Sunday	35,879

(i)   On which day did the minimum numbers of spectators see the match?

(ii)   On an average _____ spectators visited the stadium during Thursday and Friday.

(iii)   Cost of a ticket is $ 20. The money collected on Thursday and Friday is $ _____.

(iv)   How many more spectators were there on Monday than Wednesday?

(v)   Least visitors recorded on _____.

Assignment II

1. Simplify the following:

    25500 - [5100 - {2700 - (900 - 800 + 700)}]

2. What fraction of numbers located in between 1 and 20 are prime numbers?

3. Which of the following statement is not correct regarding the properties of rectangle and square?

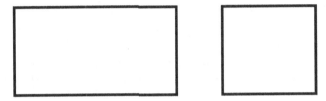

   a. Opposite sides are equal to each other.

   b. Opposite sides are parallel to each other.

   c. Interior angles are right angles.

   d. Diagonals are not equal to each other.

   e. Sum total of all the interior angles is 360^0 .

   f. Diagonals divide the shape into congruent triangles.

4. If the recipe calls for one and one-fourth cups of flour, how much flour will you use?

5. The area of a rectangular floor that is fourteen and one-half feet wide is two hundred thirty-nine and one-fourth square feet. Find the perimeter of the floor.

6. Complete the following:

$$\frac{3}{5} = \frac{}{15} = \frac{21}{} = \frac{}{45} = \frac{45}{}$$

Assignment III

1. Anamika prepares to put fencing around her rectangular kitchen garden of width 95.24 m and the length 105 m 76 cm. How long fencing wires does she need to cover the entire outer boundary leaving a 3 m broad entrance open?

    A: 400 m 200   B: 399 m   C: 202 m 2 cm   D: 397.2 m

2. Multiples of 16 are also multiples of 4 and 8, but all multiples of _____ and _____ are not multiples of 16.

3. 33% of 90.09 = _____.

4. After adding 0.125 to a decimal number the sum total becomes a decimal number having a position in the middle of 14 and 17. Find the place of that original number on the number line provided.

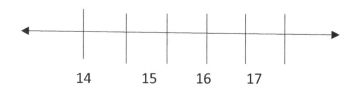

    14   15   16   17

5. A regular pentagon has __a___ lines of symmetry less than a hexagon. It has _____b _____ lines of symmetry more than an equilateral triangle. Both square and equilateral triangle has __ c__ lines of symmetry in all.

	a	b	c
A:	1	2	7
B:	2	4	8
C:	1	2	3
D:	2	4	6

6. A football is 27 times heavier than a tennis ball. A tennis ball is 9 times lighter than a rubber ball. _____ rubber balls will be equal of three footballs.

7. Other two angles of a triangle are 2/3rd and 1/3rd of a right angle respectively. Find the measure of all the interior angles of a triangle.

8. Ravi is 3 years older than Mallika but 2 years younger than Kamal. Who is youngest among them? Arrange their names in ascending order of their age.

9. Total cost of 5 pens and 3 pencils is Rs. 85. Find the total cost of 1 pen and 1 pencil if total cost of 3 pens and 2 pencils is Rs. 61.

10. 12% of 24% of 39/144 = _____.

11. A pentagon has _____ diagonals in all.

12. What must be added to make 10,982 divisible by 11?

13. Find a factor of 121 which is also a factor of 2020.

14. Difference of digits of a two digit number is 7. if digits are reversed then sum total of both the number becomes the predecessor of the three digit smallest number. Find the second multiple of this number.

    A: 45 B: 18 C: 36 D: 81

15. On Monday, Meena wanted to meet a reporter at 11.30 am sharp. Due to traffic problems she was 25 min late. Mohini left 15 min after Meena. Rebeka reported her arrival time 55 min more than that of Mohini. At what time did Rebeka reach?

    A: 1:30 pm   B: 1:40 pm   C: 11:55 am   D: 12:40 pm

16. Observe the following statements. It describes the population of cats, dogs and rabbits in a city duly recorded last year.

Number of Cats < Number of Dogs

Number of Dogs > Number of Rabbits

Which could be the number of cats and dogs?

	Cats	Dogs	Rabbits
A	192	232	176
B	306	127	176
C	432	542	675
D	541	329	767

17. A wall mount clock takes 2 seconds to ring two bells at 2 O Clock. Calculate the time taken by the same clock to ring seven bells at 7 O Clock.

A: 14 seconds   B: 7 seconds   C: 12 seconds   D: 10 seconds

18. Complete the following:

1, 4, 9, __a___, __b___, ___c___;

Options	a	b	c
A:	16	25	36
B:	21	27	29
C:	12	15	19

19. The digit at one's place of a number which is 3 less than the third multiple of 1427.

A: 6   B:7   C: 8   D: 9

20. There are two combinations of packs containing pens and pencils. Packet one containing 6 pens and 5 pencils costs Rs 128. Packet B containing 5 pens and 6 pencils costs Rs 103. Calculate the cost of a new pack containing 10 pens and 10 pencils of such type?

A: Rs. 250   B: Rs. 120   C: Rs. 135   D: Rs. 210

21. Last Thursday in the calendar it was 27th February 2020. The forthcoming Thursday will be _____ March 2020.

A: 4   B: 5   C: 6   D: 7

22. The product of 10th multiple of 11 and the 7th multiple of 109 has _____ at its one's place.

A: 0   B: 1   C: 2   D: 3

23. 121, 169 and 219 have following things in common:

I. All these numbers are square numbers.

II. These are square numbers of odd primes.

III. These numbers have equal numbers of prime factors.

Select which of the statements mentioned above are true.

A: Only I   B: Only II   C: Both I and III   D: All I, II and III

24. The number thirtysix has _____ factors in all:

Statement   : 36 is a composite numbers.

Reason   : 36 has more than two factors.

A: The given reason is appropriate.

B: The given reason is not correct.

C: The given reason requires more explanation.

D: Both the statement and reason are wrong.

25. Observe following statements:

I: 2 is an even prime number.

II: 2 has no factors other than 1 and the number itself.

III: 2 has another factor which is also a factor of all the other natural numbers.

IV: All the other even numbers are multiples of 2.

Select which of the statements mentioned above are true.

A: Only I   B: Only II   C: Only I and III   D: All

26. A train can cross a telephone post in 45 seonds while moving at an average speed of 20 m /s. find length of the train.

27. What least number must be added to a five digit smallest number to make it multiple of 9?

3. Model Paper

1. A map scale designates 1" = 50 miles. If the distance between two towns on the map is 2.75 inches, how many miles must you drive to go from the first town to the second?

2. . Bob is taking his son to look at colleges. The first college they plan to visit is 150 miles from their home. In the first hour they drive at a rate of 60 mph. If they want to reach their destination in 2 ½ hours, what speed must they average for the remainder of their trip?

3. Four employees can wash 20 service vehicles in 5 hours. How long would it take 5 employees to wash the same number of vehicles?

4. A can do a work in 8 days and B can do the same work in 12 days. Both A and B jointly can do the same work in _____ days.

5. For every 1^0 C increase of temperature there is 1.8^0 F increase. A weather report of a city exhibited difference of maximum and minimum temperature by 36.9^0 F. find the corresponding difference in Celsius scale.

6. In the last three years, Frederico's basketball team won 30 more games than they lost. If they won 150 games, what was their ratio of wins to losses? Show the ratio in three different ways.

7. 150 men jointly can finish a work in 20 days. How many more men can join the team to finish the same work in 16 days?

8. Half of a quarter of 192.192 = _____.

9. Ruchira got 139 in an examinations and scored 4 marks more than her friend Kim. The score of Kim was 90% of the full marks. Find the score of Ruchira in percentage.

10. What least number must be subtracted from a seven digit greatest number to make it a multiple of 4?

   a. Step I---We subtract the remainder from the seven digit number.

   b. Step II -- For Working out this value we can make a two digit number formed by taking digits of tens and one's place.

   c. Step III -- We check the divisibility of this 2 digit number by 4.

   d. Step IV--Result will be displayed.

   If these steps arranged properly then the sequence of steps will be..

      A: a,c,b,d

      B: b,c,ad

      C: c,a,b,d

11. Pinki wanted to add three digit greatest number and a successor of five digit greatest number. The sum total of digits in hundreds, thousands and ten thousands place present in the sum total is _____.

12. What least number can be subtracted from each of the following values to make them multiple of 11?

   126; 12,326; 1,234,326; 5,560 and 6,671

13. Observe the Prime Factorisations:

   a) 121   =   1 X 11 X 11;

b) 144 = 1 X 12 X 12;

c) 169 = 1 X 13 X 13;

d) 101 = 1 X 101;

e) 196 = 1 X 14 X 14;

f) 225 = 1 X 15 X 15;

Statements:

I. All the numbers displayed above are square numbers having only three factors.

II. 1 comes as a factor in the prime factorisation of all natural numbers.

III. None of the numbers displayed above are prime numbers.

IV. Number having only two factors, 1 and the number itself, is called a prime number.

Is there any wrong statement?

Options:

A: Only I and II are wrong.

B: Only III and V are wrong.

C: Only III is wrong.

D: Only II, III and V are wrong.

14. If 109X 11 = 1199 then,

a. $1.09 \times 1.1 =$ _____.

b. $10.9 \times 0.11 =$ _____.

c. $109 \times 0.011 =$ _____ .

d. $0.109 \times 11 =$ _____.

Statements:

I. Values of product in all the four cases are same.

II. All the four products have same places of decimals.

III. Products in all the four cases will be rounded up to nearest whole number as 12.

IV. There is no similarity in products in all the four cases.

Which of the above statements are not correct?

Options:

A: I and II   B : III and IV   C : All   D: None

15. There are two combinations of packs containing Cakes and Biscuits. Packet one containing 6 cakes and 5 biscuitsls costs Rs 128. Packet B containing 5 cakes and 6 biscuits costs Rs 103. Calculate the cost of a new pack containing 10 cakes and 10 biscuits of such type?

A: Rs. 250   B: Rs. 120

C: Rs. 135   D: Rs. 210

16. What fraction of numbers starting from 1 to 40 are prime numbers?

17. Observe the following statements. It describes the population of cats, dogs and rabbits in a city duly recorded last year.

a. Number of Cats < Number of Dogs

b. Number of Dogs > Number of Rabbits

Which could be the number of cats and dogs?

	Cats	Dogs	Rabbits
A	192	232	176
B	306	127	176
C	432	542	675
D	541	329	767

18.. A wall mount clock takes 2 seconds to ring two bells at 2 O Clock. Calculate the time taken by the same clock to ring seven bells at 7 O Clock.

A: 14 seconds   B: 7 seconds

C: 12 seconds   D: 10 seconds

19. Complete the following:

1, 4, 9, __a___, __b___, ___c___;

Options	a	b	c
A:	16	25	36
B:	21	27	29
C:	12	15	19

20. Find the least number of five digits divisible exactly by 5, 12 and 16 exactly without leaving any remainder.

21.The digit at one's place of a number which is 3 less than the third multiple of 1427.

A: 6   B:7   C: 8   D: 9

22. There are two combinations of packs containing pens and pencils. Packet one containing 6 pens and 5 pencils costs Rs 128. Packet B containing 5 pens and 6 pencils costs Rs 103. Calculate the cost of a new pack containing 10 pens and 10 pencils of such type?

    A: Rs. 250   B: Rs. 120

    C: Rs. 135   D: Rs. 210

23. Last Thursday in the calendar it was 27th February 2020. The forthcoming Thursday will be _____March 2020.

    A: 4   B: 5

    C: 6   D: 7

24. The product of 10th multiple of 11 and the 7th multiple of 109 has _____ at its one's place.

    A: 0   B: 1   C: 2   D: 3

25. 121, 169 and 219 have following things in common:

    I. All these numbers are square numbers.

    II. These are square numbers of odd primes.

    III. These numbers have equal numbers of prime factors.

    Select which of the statements mentioned above are true.

    A: Only I   B: Only II

    C: Both I and III   D: All I, II and III

26. 144 has _____ factors in all:

    Statement : 144 is a composite numbers.

    Reason   : 144 has more than two factors.

A: The given reason is appropriate.

B: The given reason is not correct.

C: The given reason requires more explanation.

D: Both the statement and reason are wrong.

27. Observe following statements:

I: 2 is an even prime number.

II: 2 has no factors other than 1 and the number itself.

III: 2 has another factor which is also a factor of all the other natural numbers.

IV: All the other even numbers are multiples of 2.

Select which of the statements mentioned above are true.

A: Only I   B: Only II

C: Only I and III   D: All

28. How many non-overlapping triangles can be fitted inside a hexagon?

29. There are _____ faces and _____ edges in a pentagonal prism.

30. Calculate the least number which can be subtracted from 258,129,132 to make it a multiple of 129.

4. Evaluation

1. Evaluate the following expressions:

a.
$$\frac{\dfrac{101}{119}X\dfrac{238}{43}X43}{\dfrac{121}{101}}+\frac{21}{101}+\frac{19}{101}= \ldots\ldots$$

b.
$$\frac{\dfrac{11}{19}X\dfrac{38}{43}X\dfrac{43}{121}X\dfrac{19}{200}}{101}+\frac{21}{101}+\frac{19}{101}= \ldots\ldots$$

c. $=$
$$\frac{\dfrac{19}{109}+\dfrac{43}{109}+\dfrac{101}{218}}{101}+\frac{101}{211}+\frac{109}{211}= \ldots\ldots$$

2. Convert into decimal

a. $\dfrac{101}{25} = \underline{\hspace{3cm}}$

b. $\dfrac{7}{18}+\dfrac{1}{36}+\dfrac{3}{18} = \underline{\hspace{2cm}}$

c. $\dfrac{101}{25} = \underline{\hspace{2cm}}$

d. $\dfrac{211}{18} = \underline{\hspace{2cm}}$

3. What is the reciprocal of $(0.125)^{-1/2}$?

6. Complete the Chart...

Standard Form	Expanded Form
1020.3257	$1 \times 1000 + 2 \times 10 + \dfrac{3}{10} + \dfrac{2}{100} + \dfrac{5}{1000} + \dfrac{7}{10000}$
109.109	
	2 hundreds + 21 tens + 19 tenths + 19 thousandths

7. Write in Standard form :

    a. 4,308.3048 =

    b. 32 hundredth + 121 thousandths=

8. If $\dfrac{2}{5}\ of\ 40 = \dfrac{2}{5} \times 40 = \dfrac{2 \times 40}{5} = 2 \times 8 = 16$

    a. What is $\dfrac{3}{5}of\ 60$?

9. Add : $\dfrac{2}{10} + \dfrac{33}{100} + \dfrac{121}{1000} + \dfrac{6}{5}$

10. 19 + 19 tenths + 19 thousandths = _____.

11. $3\dfrac{1}{2} + 11\dfrac{7}{8} =$

12. Half of a quarter of 64 = _____.

13.Multiply : $\dfrac{10}{121} X \dfrac{11}{100} X \dfrac{13}{24} X \dfrac{11}{26} X \dfrac{4}{5} =$

14.Tap A can fill up a water tank in 30 minutes and tap B can empty the same water tank in 45 minutes. Tap A will take _____ minutes to fill the tank when both the taps remain open.

15. A cistern can fill a water tank in 45 minutes and a tap can empty the same water tank in 1 hour 30 minutes. Find the time taken up by the cistern to fill the tank when the tap kept open.

16. Three triangles joined side by side to form a polygon having ___ sides. Sum total of all the interior angles of this polygon is _____^{0}.

[Angle Sum Property of a Triangle: Sum total of all the interior angles of a triangle is 180^0.]

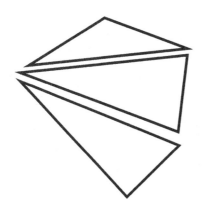

17. Mohanlal deposited a sum of Rs. 65,000 in a bank for a tenure of 5 years at a simple rate of interest and received Rs 80,000 after the maturity. Find the rate of simple interest offered by the bank.

18. Observe the figure:

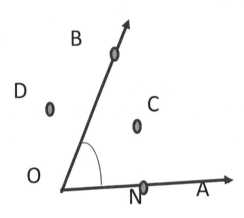

Complete the following:

a) Write names of different rays present in the given figure. Example: **OB**

b) There are _____ arms and _____ vertex.

c) _____ and _____ are two arms of this angle.

d) Point _____ is lying inside the angle.

e) Name of this angle is _____.

f) Two rays meeting at a point. This point is called _____ of the angle.

g) Point _____ and _____ are lying on the angle.

h) Point _____ is lying at the exterior of the angle.

i) Point _____ is lying in the interior of the angle.

j) < AOB is an angle because:

I.   It has two _____ ;

II. It has a _____ ;

III. It has a definite_____ .

19. Fill in the blanks:

    a. A triangle having _____ right angles is not possible.

    b. A triangle having _____ obtuse angles is not possible.

    c. Sum total of all the interior angles of a polygon is 540^0. Find the number of sides it has. There are _____ diagonals in this polygon.

    d. Sum total of all the interior angles of a polygon is equal to four right angles. It must have at least one _____ angle or at least _____ right angles. They cannot have less than _____ obtuse angles.

    e. Identify following triangles:

    f. Supplementary angle of complementary angle of 56^0 is equal to

    _____.

    g. A quadrilateral having maximum number of _____ right angles is possible.

    h. What fraction of right angle is 30^0?

    i. A quadrilateral having maximum number of _____ acute angles is possible.

    j. A triangle having two _____ angles or two _____ angles is not possible.

20. Find the number of triangles in each figure.

| I | II | III | IV |

I. Number of triangles increases from figure I onwards in a definite incremental pattern.

II. This incremental pattern can be continued by adding next natural number.

III. In the same incremental pattern 6th figure will represent 21 triangles in all.

IV. This pattern has no definite incremental value for each step.

Which of the statements regarding the pattern of triangles are not true?

A: Only I   B: I, II and III

C: III and IV   D: Only IV

21. If 5% of 5% of 16 = $\dfrac{16}{25} = \dfrac{16 X 4}{25 X 4} = \dfrac{64}{100} = 0.64$, then calculate the value of 4% of 5% of 19.

22. Area of each white tiles in the pattern is 25 cm². white tiles are arranged in a uniform sequential pattern. Length of this shape is _____ cm, its breadth is _____ cm and area is _____ square cm.

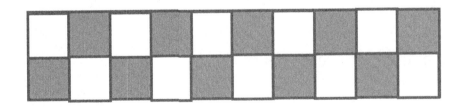

23. 27 tenths + 43 hundredths + 13 tens = _____.

24. 121.121 ÷ 11 = P;   P X 1,000 = Q;

$$\frac{P}{Q} + \frac{Q}{P} = R$$

I. R is a decimal number and can be expressed into an improper fraction and also can be represented in the form of a mixed number.

II. Value of R has three decimal places. It can be rounded down to nearest thousand for obtaining the four digit smallest number.

III. Decimal part of R is equal to 10 ten thousandths.

Which of the above mentioned statements regarding the value of R are not true?

A: Only I   B: only II   C: None   D: All

25. Identify the following figures:

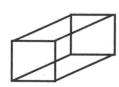 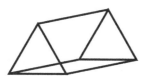

Name: _____   _____   _____

Faces (F)   ____   _____   _____

Edges: (E)   ____   _____   _____

Corners (V) ____   _____   _____

F +V – E =   ____   _____   _____

From the above observation find the following:

a) Is it possible to draw a polygon having 2 faces, 2 vertices and 5 edges?

b) Can you draw a triangle having 6 edges, 4 faces and 4 vertices? If yes, identify the same.

Euler stressed on uses of five major components of a polyhedron in

105

an effort to establish a relationship between them.
  i.   **Vertices**, (a location where 2 or more edges meet),
  ii. **Faces** (contained and defined by 3 or more edges),
  iii. **Edges** (defined as the "ridge or sharp edge"[2] of a polyhedron),
  iv. **Sides** (used to refer to the sides of each face),
  v.   **Plane angles** (the angle found at a vertex, contained by 2 sides).

26. A plot located in the front side of the residence of Mohan is rectangular in size. He has planted saplings in his front side plot at an interval of 2 m with uniformity in between 6 rows and 20 columns. Calculate the number of saplings Mohan arranged for this activity. Find the dimension of that plot.

27. The cost of tiling a square sized floor of side 6 m at the rate of Rs. 5 per square cm is Rs. _____.

28. A 1200 cm long wire is to be reshaped in rectangular form. Find the maximum possible and minimum possible length of that rectangle.

29. Mohan, Ravi, Kanika and Maneka are standing at four vertices of a rectangle having length 200 m and breadth 80 m. distance between Mohan and Ravi is greater than that of Kanika, but greatest distant from him is Maneka. Identify the types of intermediate distances in between these friends in terms of length, breadth and diagonals. Which of distances indicate diagonals of the rectangular shape?

30. Identify all the rays represented in the given line.

31. Supplementary angle of certain given angle is 145⁰.

     i.   Find the complementary angles.

     ii.   Sum total of supplementary and complementary angle is _____.

32. < BOC is a right angle.
     Supplement of <1 =

     Find two sets of linear pair.

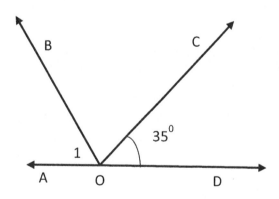

33. What must be added to a six digit greatest number to make it a seven digit smallest multiple of 18?

34. Exterior angles of a polygon are 1st , 2nd 3rd and 4th multiple of 36^0. Find all the interior angles of this polygon.

    [Exterior angle along with corresponding interior angle of any polygon are supplementary to each other.]

35. Interior angles of a triangle are first second and third multiples of 30^0. Find the angles. What is the special name of that triangle?

36. Observe the following diagram.

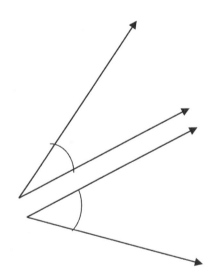

a. Pair of angles displayed here are non-adjacent angles.

b. These angles have uncommon vertex and uncommon arms.

c. None of the conditions for becoming adjacent angles are fulfilled by these angles.

d. These angles may represent a complementary pair.

e. If rays propagating parallel to each other fuses then the pair may become an adjacent pair.

Which of the statements are not properly projected for describing nature and magnitude of these angles.

A: Only IV   B: IV and V   C: III and V

5. Additional Activities

Name all the possible angles in the following figures.

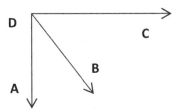

2. Write the missing angle in the following groups representing angles of a triangle.

a. 32^0 , _____, 78^0 b. 52^0 , _____, 98^0 c. 132^0 , _____, 18^0

3. Two concentric circles of radii 14 cm and 7 cm encloses a definite area. Find the area enclosed by outer boundaries of both the circle.

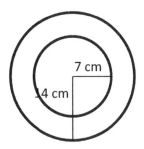

4. Study the diagram and answer the questions.

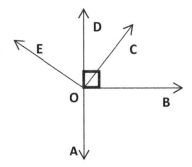

a) Name a right angle, a straight angle and two acute angles,

b) Write the measure of <AOB.

c) Which angle is complementary to <DOC ?

5. Fill in the blanks:

a) The number 365 is divisible by both _____ and _____.

b) The number 121 has two factors other than 1. Those two factors are _____ and _____.

c) Product of two numbers is 284. Their HCF is 132 and LCM is _____.

d) There are _____ diagonals in a hexagon.

e) We can subtract _____ and _____ from 134,000 and 129,000,000 respectively to make them exactly divisible by 11.

6. Complete the following:

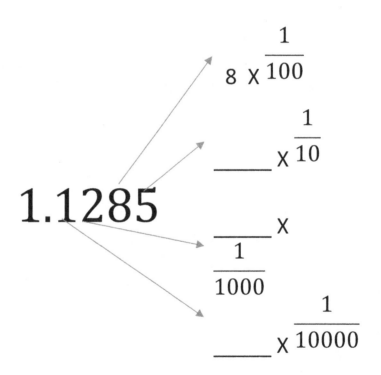

$$8 \times \frac{1}{100}$$

$$\_\_\_\_ \times \frac{1}{10}$$

$$\_\_\_\_ \times \frac{1}{1000}$$

$$1.1285$$

$$\_\_\_\_ \times \frac{1}{10000}$$

7. What percentage of numbers starting from 1 to 50 are prime numbers?

8. Which number is a reciprocal of itself?

Projects and Handouts

Complete the following Expansion Chart

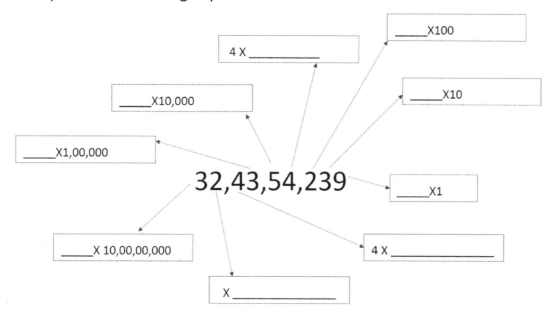

1. Complete the following:

   a) Numbers divisible by 2 are also called _____ numbers.

   b) _____ is the only even prime number.

   c) All prime numbers have only _____ factors. _____ and the number itself.

   d) Sum total of 2 eve numbers is always an _____ number.

   e) Sum total of an even number and an odd number is always an _____ number.

   f) A prime number between 95 and 100 = _____.

   g) All the multiples of 8 are also multiples of 2 and _____.

   h) All the multiples of _____ and 4 may or may not be a multiple of 8.

   i) All the multiples of ____ and _____ are not necessarily multiples of 10.

   j) All multiples of 10 are also multiples of _____ and _____.

2. Answer the following:

   a. What least number must be added to 109 to make it a multiple of 3?

   b. Identify 4 pairs of twin prime numbers.

   c. Find a pair of twin prime number whose sum total is 300.

   d. Find the sum total of a twin prime numbers which is also a multiple of 4.

   e. How many twin primes are there in between 1 and 20?

   f. Which prime numbers are predecessor and successor of 100?

   g. Consecutive primes located just before 200 are _____ and _____.

   h. Subtract 546, 435 from 6 million.

   i. What must be added to 6 million to make it the greatest 7 digit number?

3. Add the following.

43,432	87,890	76,809
+32,765	+54,654	+43,659
+43,435	+78,657	+101,101
+119,632	+607,700	+405,607

4. Rishabh covered a 400 m hardles in 49 seconds and defeated his counterpart by a gap of 3.5 seconds. Find the average speed of both the athlete.

5. Simplify:

$$\frac{1}{2} \times \frac{2}{3} \times \frac{3}{4} \times \frac{4}{5} \times \frac{5}{6} \times \ldots\ldots \frac{999}{1000} = \underline{\hspace{2cm}}.$$

6. Answer the following:

A. Add the following:

    i.   123,433,540 + 32,435+ 324,435

    ii.   101,101 + 320,239 + 101,909 + 202,208

    iii.   3 million + 324 thousand + 324 hundred

    iv.   21 million + 213 thousand + 213

    v.   21X 10,000 + 21 X 20,000 + 11X 10,000

    vi.   21X 10,000 + 21X 1,--- + 21X 100

    vii.   32 lakhs + 324 thousands + 21 hundreds + 21 tens

B. You are selling drinks at the school dance. You have a cooler, which holds 35 cups. The canteen gets busy and you lose track of how many cups you sold. You check and see that there are 17 cups left in the cooler. How many drinks must you have sold?

C. Rani is buying light bulbs for her Christmas decorations. She buys 1020 but when she gets to the cash, she has to put back 3 hundred 13 because they are broken. How many light bulbs does Marie buy?

D. <1 = <2 = <COD. Find the supplementary angle of <1.
   a) Identify two pairs of adjacent angles.
   b) Reflex angle of <2 = _____.
   c) <AOD = _____.
   d) Reflex angle of <AOD = __.
   e) Supplement of <2 = _____.

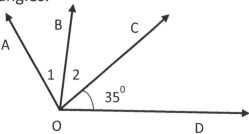

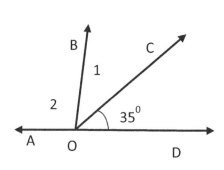

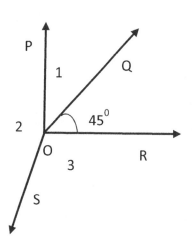

E. OC bisects <BOD.
<1 = _____;
<2 = _____;
Identify 2 sets of linear pairs.

F. <1 = 2/3rd of <QOR
   <2 = 5 times <1;
   Find all the angles.

G. A regular hexagon has _____ diagonals. Its interior angles are equal in magnitude. Sum total of all the interior angles is _____.

H. Find the least number of three digits which can be subtracted from the greatest seven digit number to make that number divisible by 4.

I. 20% of _____ = 120.45.

J. Observe the chart of Roman Numerals:

117

I	II	III	IV	V
1	2	3	4	5
VI	VII	VIII	IX	X
6	7	8	9	10
L	C	D	M	
50	100	500	1,000	

Examples:

MMCXLII　　=　　MM　+ CC　XL　　III

2, 243 =　　　2 X 1000　　+ 2 X 100　　+ 4 X 10　　　+ 3

Complete the following:

MMXVI　　　=　　MM + ... X　　VI

2, 016 =　　　.... X 1000　　+ ..... X 100　　+ .... X 10　　　+ ....

Complete the following:

_____　　　=　　　_____+ ___ + XC　+___

1,994 =　　　...... X 1000 + ... X 100 + ... X 10　　　+ ....

Find the value:

1. MMMCMLXXXIX　　=
2. Find the value of 2020 in Roman numerals.

K. Answer the following:

1. Find a smallest number which can divide a greatest 5 digit number leaving remainder 11.

2. Find a greatest number which can divide 8,081, 6,434, 5,453 and 4,679 leaving remainder 8 in each case.

3. What must be added to the greatest 6 digit number to make it divisible by 8?

4. Find LCM of all the three numbers formed by using digits 5,4 and 0 only once.

5. What least number must be added to make 20,432 divisible by 9?

6. Three buses stop at intervals of 210 m, 510 m and 850 m respectively. Find the intervals having common stoppage for all the three buses.

7. Rohit started dividing 2015, 3022 and 5,061 by a same divisor. There was remainders 7, 6 and 5 respectively. Find the greatest possible divisor of such type.

8. Milton and Radha got same marks in Mathematics. Both the marks are in between 75 and 90. their marks is also a multiple of 11. find their marks.

9. Blue green and red ropes of 220 m, 380 m and 460 m were used for obtaining similar small cut pieces of equal size. Find the maximum possible size of each cut pieces. Also find the total number of cut pieces of that size.

10. Is 32,324,43 divisible by 11? If not, what least number can be subtracted to make it divisible by 11?

Add On Papers 001

1. $\dfrac{1}{10} + \dfrac{3}{100} + \dfrac{11}{10000} + \dfrac{121}{1000} =$ _____

2. $\dfrac{21}{10} + \dfrac{43}{100} + \dfrac{321}{10000} + \dfrac{3241}{1000} =$ _____

3. 132.043 = _____ + ____ tenths + ____ hundredths + _____

   thousandths.

4. 32.104 = _____ + ____ tenths + ____ hundredths + _____

   thousandths.

5. _____ = 1029 + 21 tenths + 321 hundredths + 1209

   thousandths.

6. Arrange in ascending order:

   a) $2\dfrac{3}{4}, 2\dfrac{4}{3}, 2\dfrac{8}{9}, 2\dfrac{17}{18}$

   b) $29\%, 2.09, \dfrac{29}{1000}, \dfrac{2.9}{100}, \dfrac{0.29}{100}, 20\% \ of \ 58, 5\% \ of \ 290$

   c) $35\%, 3.5, \dfrac{0.35}{100}, 35X\dfrac{1}{100}, 50 \% \ 0f \ 700, 25\% \ 0f \ 140, 7th \ mult$

   d) 390, 39%, 3,902, 39 hundredths of 3,000, 39th multiple of

   100.

   e) 121, 121 hundredths, 1,21 tenths, 0.121 tenths, 121

   hundredths.

Add On Papers 002

1. Last Thursday in the calendar it was 27th February 2020. The forthcoming Thursday will be _____March 2020.

   A: 4   B: 5

   C: 6   D: 7

2. The product of 10th multiple of 11 and the 7th multiple of 109 has _____ at its one's place.

   A: 0   B: 1

   C: 2   D: 3

3. Difference of digits of a two digit number is 7. if digits are reversed then sum total of both the number becomes the predecessor of the three digit smallest number. Find the second multiple of this number.

4. Compare the place value of 3 in 2,309 and 3,283. Find the difference of both the place values of 3. The difference is the _(____) th multiple of 100.

5. 121, 169 and 219 have following things in common:

I. All these numbers are square numbers.

II. These are square numbers of odd primes.

III. These numbers have equal numbers of prime factors.

Select which of the statements mentioned above are true.

A: Only I   B: Only II

C: Both I and III   D: All

6. Complete the Prime factorisation:

a) 141   = ___ X___;

b) 84 = _____;

c) 363 = _____ X _____ ;

d) 3,000 = 2 X 2 X 2 X _____

e) 729 = _ X __X___ X ___X__;

f) _____ = 89 X 11

7. In the calculation table depicted below numbers are related to each other. Find their inter relations and also identify missing numbers.

8. 32 X 10,000

= _____ X 16 = _____ X 8.

9. 8th multiple of of 16 is _____ multiple of 32.

10. 9th multiple of 11 is _____ multiple of 9.

11. After subtracting _____ we can obtain 3rd multiple of 13 from the 4th multiple of 10.

12. Complete the following:

f) 1, 4, 9, __i___, __ii___, _iii_;

g) i X ii + iii = _____

h) 1, 8, 27, ____, ___ __ , __ _ .

i) 121, ___, _____ , _____ 161.

j) 64, _____, _____ , _____ , 16, 9.

13. Product of all the factors of 6 = _____

    A: 36   B: 12

    C: 18   D: 24

14. How many diagonals are there in a pentagon?

15. Rohan added 2001 to a number instead of subtracting 201 from that number. Find the difference of his actual and desired result.

16. What least number should be added to the seven digit smallest number to make it a dividend of 11 and 2?

17. Some of the statements regarding prime and composite numbers are given below.

    I : 1 is not a prime *or* composite number.

    II : Two is the only even prime number.

    III: All odd numbers are not prime.

    IV: All composite numbers can be written as product of prime numbers.

    V: 101 has only two factors 1 and the number itself. That is why it is a prime number

    Which of the above statements are true?

A: Only I

B: All

C: I, II and III

D: II, III and IV

Addon Paper 004

1. Rohit had a candy bar divided into 16 equal parts. He gave 3 pieces to Kamalika and 2 pieces to Mohan. What fraction of Candy bar is left with him?

2. While calculating perimeter of her garden Ratna calculated the length and breadth of the garden. It was 1500 m long and 600 m wide. _____ times the sum total of length and _____ will be the perimeter of the garden. Find the perimeter in km.

3. For a punch bowl, Carin needs a block of ice with a volume of at least 125 cubic inches. She has a cube of ice that is five inches on each side. Write the volume of the cube using a base and exponents. Then write it in standard form. Is the block of ice big enough? Remember that volume is calculated by multiplying length times width times height.

4. Tickets to the school play cost Rs 300 for adults and Rs 200 for students. If 235 adults and 322 students attended the play, write an expression that shows the total amount of money made on ticket sales. Then simplify the expression.

5. Observe the following:

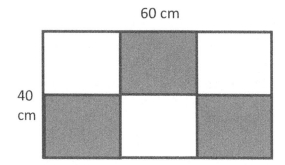

60 cm

40 cm

A rectangular floor has three square tiles of side 20 cm each.   The area remained uncovered is _____ cm2

I: it is equivalent to 12 tiles of 100 cm^2 each.

II: It is half of the area covered by tiles.

III: It requires same number of tiles as previously used.

Which of the statements are true?

A: Only II and III   B: Only II

C: All   D: None

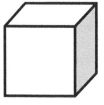

Fig 1

6. Observe the following figure:

There are two solid shapes

Fig 1 is a cube and Fig 2 is a cylinder.

I: Fig 2 has a curved face.

II: Fig 1 has six flat faces in all.

III: Fig 2 has 4 flat faces less than

that of flat faces.

Fig 2

IV: Fig 2 resembles a cylinder.

V: Fig 1 has 8 corners.

VI: Top view of Fig 1 is a square.

Which of the above statements

regarding solid shapes are true?

A: Only I and II   B: Only III   C: All   D: None

7. There are three cylindrical containers.

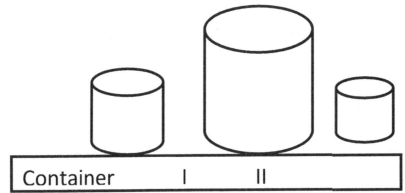

Container II holds 10 times more water than that of I. Container II is three times bigger in volume than that of III.

If we use the smallest container for filling up both I and II, then we have to use it for ____times.

A: 30   B: 33   C: 36   D: 48

8. In 45,657 sum total of place values of 5 = _____

 A: 25

B: 50,500

C: 550

D: 5,050

9. During vacation you spent Rs 127 out of Rs 250. There was another 500 rupees note with you. Find the money left with you.

10. Shapes below shows a definite pattern:

Made in the USA
Monee, IL
28 January 2023

26548124R00070